VENICE

By Aubrey Menen
and the Editors of Time-Life Books

Photographs by Ernst Haas

THE GREAT CITIES · TIME-LIFE BOOKS · AMSTERDAM

The Author: Aubrey Menen was born in London of Indian/Irish parentage. He attended University College London, where H. G. Wells encouraged him to become a writer. He became a director of London's Experimental Theatre for which he wrote and produced several plays. For the last twenty years he has devoted his time entirely to writing. Among his best known books are, *Rome Revealed, The Prevalence of Witches* and *The Duke of Gallodoro.*

The Photographer: Ernst Haas was born in Vienna in 1921. He became interested in photography during the Second World War, and in 1947 his work was exhibited for the first time, in Vienna. Since then he has had several other shows, including one at New York's Museum of Modern Art. His photographs have appeared in LIFE, numerous magazines and books.

THE GREAT CITIES
Editor: Dale Brown
Design Consultant: Louis Klein
Picture Editor: Pamela Marke
Assistant Picture Editor: Anne Angus

Editorial Staff for Venice
Designer: Graham Davis
Staff Writer: Deborah Thompson
Picture Researcher: Jasmine Spencer
Text Researchers: Vanessa Kramer, Jackie Matthews
Design Assistant: Shirin Patel

Editorial Production for the Series
Art Department: Susan Goldblatt
Editorial Department: Julia West, Betty H. Weatherley
Picture Department: Cathy Doxat-Pratt, Christine Hinze

The captions and text of the picture essays were written by the staff of TIME-LIFE Books

Valuable assistance was given in the preparation of this volume by TIME-LIFE Correspondent Ann Natanson, Rome

Published by TIME-LIFE International (Nederland) B.V.
Ottho Heldringstraat 5, Amsterdam 1018

Cover: Gondolas ride their own reflections in a Venetian canal. By tradition the six prongs on their prows represent Venice's six districts.

First end paper: The façade of the Palace of the Doges, the seat of government in the old Venetian Republic, is seen through a café's flowery curtain. The resulting image captures delicately the tone of Venice today.

Last end paper: Brass sea horses and coloured cushions brighten a rank of sombre gondolas, which have been painted black since an edict was issued in 1562 to curb the ostentation of rich Venetians.

THE WORLD'S WILD PLACES
HUMAN BEHAVIOUR
THE ART OF SEWING
THE OLD WEST
THE EMERGENCE OF MAN
LIFE LIBRARY OF PHOTOGRAPHY
TIME-LIFE LIBRARY OF ART
FOODS OF THE WORLD
GREAT AGES OF MAN
LIFE SCIENCE LIBRARY
LIFE NATURE LIBRARY

Contents

1 | **The Gift of Venice** | 5
Picture essay: A City Awash | 20

2 | **Glorious Shadows of the Past** | 31
Picture essay: Treasure House of Colour | 44

3 | **A Flair for the Theatrical** | 57
Picture essay: Regal Day on the Grand Canal | 68

4 | **Signs of Change** | 81

5 | **A Delight to the Eye** | 95
Picture essay: Reflected Glory | 108

6 | **An Artistic Legacy** | 117
Picture essay: An Added Attraction—the Tourists | 130

7 | **A Faded Splendour** | 143
Picture essay: The Seagirt Satellites | 154

8 | **Surviving the Present** | 169
Picture essay: The Ephemeral Venice | 188

Acknowledgements and Bibliography | 198

Index | 199

I

The Gift of Venice

Venice is the most beautiful city in the world. Yet in describing it to you, I have a difficulty. I fear you will be bored. Many people do get bored with Venice, precisely because it is so very beautiful. They do not like to say so, because a visit to Venice costs a great deal of money, and nobody likes to spend money to be bored. But the Venetians know all about it, and do not want visitors to stay too long, anyway. It could well have been the Venetians who coined that telling phrase: "Guests are like fish. After three days, they stink."

Let me try to explain the difficulty by describing what happened when I met Sophia Loren. In 1966 Sophia was generally acknowledged to be one of the most beautiful women in the world. In this regard there was no challenge to her supremacy, just as there is no challenge to the supremacy of Venice. So I decided I would go out of my way to meet Sophia and look at her, much as I would go out of my way to see the Taj Mahal.

The thing was arranged. I journeyed deep into the south of Italy, where she was making a film. I stayed at the same hotel, and met her many times. We talked; I watched her work; I rode beside her in her car. She was every bit as beautiful as I had thought she would be.

On the third day she gave me a very searching look and then invited me to have a tête-à-tête lunch with her. We retired to her caravan which she used on location and there, across a narrow table, talked about many things. When lunch was done, she said: "You are bored with looking at me." Before I could protest, she swept on, "So I am now going to show you all the things that are wrong with my face." With that she called her maid, who handed her some sticks of make-up. Then across the small table, she demonstrated each of her imperfections—and not until I had agreed that they were indeed faults did she cover them with touches of grease-paint.

Of course, she was quite right. Lovely as she was, I was getting tired of her. Keats wrote that a thing of beauty is a joy forever. It most decidedly is not. I have mentioned the Taj Mahal: a second visit to that monument is always a disappointment because it is flawless. One finds one's attention wandering to the monkeys that swarm in the grounds. But I go back again and again to St. Patrick's Cathedral in New York because it has so many things wrong with it. I discover a new one every visit, but I like the church more and more. I have just seen a re-run on television of the film I had watched Sophia Loren make. She seemed to me lovelier than ever.

So in describing Venice I shall praise it but I shall also criticize it, for it is the defects that only make the beautiful city less boring. For example, the

Early morning fog drains colour from St. Mark's Square and heightens the stark geometry of the lofty Campanile. On the right, stretching towards the cathedral in the background, stands the ruler-straight frontage of the Procuratie Nuove, built in the 16th Century for the Procurators, senior officials of the republic.

Palace of the Doges has earned the astonished admiration of centuries of visitors. I trust I shall not spoil your pleasure when I point out that the windows of the façade are on an uneven plane. So are Sophia's eyes.

Venice is an island. In fact it is an archipelago, but the small islands have become satellites of the big one, the Rialto; and that, in turn, is not so very big. Once around its perimeter is only eight and a half miles; the entire island is just two and a half square miles. Not that it is actually square. The island is shaped rather like a dolphin, with its mouth towards the mainland and its tail towards the open sea. Down the middle of this dolphin runs a curving canal, the dolphin's gullet, as it were; and there are two tailfins.

Now it would seem to be easy to find your way about an island small enough to be strolled round in a day and crossed in a morning. It would seem simple to arrive, walk about where you wish and come back to where you started from. If you try it in Venice, you will most certainly get lost. I can find my way about the ancient centre of Rome and even the souks of Algiers; but I have often been lost in Venice. Nor does map-reading help. The only thing to do is to ask a Venetian, who, leading you in what appears to be exactly the opposite direction to the one you had in mind, will walk you to where you want to go.

I get lost because Venice is so beautiful that I am constantly staring about me. Still, as with a beautiful woman, Venice has its imperfections. And Venice cannot mask some of them as easily as a woman. The visitor's first impression as he approaches the city through the surrounding slums is of Venice at her worst—in a shabby dressing-gown and with her hair in curlers. Therefore, let us approach Venice in the manner and style of the privileged few: from the sea, in a sleek yacht. I did it once, many years ago as a guest on one, and that is the way it should always be done.

She rises, like Venus, from the waters. If it is evening, we signal for the engines to be throttled back, so that they do not make too much noise. Gliding as though in a gondola, we watch towers and domes grow before us, their heads in the sky, their feet in the water. Long, low palaces, with pointed arches like mosques, begin to appear, one of them an unbelievable pink that seems caught from the sunset. Over all rises a tall tower, much taller than any other, and high above the domes. Again we think of Muslim lands, with their minarets for the call to prayer. We anchor in a lagoon, lower the launch and go in towards the island. It stretches out a welcoming finger—a landing place—and we tie up to it. We walk a few steps, and Venice suddenly engulfs us.

We are on great steps of white marble. At the top of them is an entrance shaped like a Roman triumphal arch; yet above that rises two domes such as the Romans, great architects as they were, could never have conceived. Just in the way we have tied up our boat, so immense stone volutes, looking like slices of Swiss roll, tie down the great dome to the walls; and the dome is so light in the air that it looks as though it needs this anchoring.

In this tempera painting completed in 1345 by Paolo Veneziano, one of the earliest of the major Venetian painters, St. Mark, the patron saint of Venice, appears twice. According to legend, when the body of St. Mark (inside the coffin) was stolen from heathen Alexandria by devout Venetians in the 9th Century, the ship bringing it back to Venice was saved from destruction in a storm only by the miraculous intervention of the saint himself (left).

This is the church of Santa Maria della Salute. It is the most stupendous entrance to any city ever conceived. Rome's Porta del Popolo and Bombay's Gateway to India were both put up to welcome monarchs, and both are very fine. But they look timid and retiring compared to this great, white, rolling, billowing masterpiece of a church. It was the last great building the Venetians put up, and it is easy to see that they had not much hope of doing anything that would better it.

We shall now approach Venice the other way, through the dolphin's mouth (Santa Maria della Salute is under his belly). It is the way most people come—and because of this, Venice, unlike Sophia Loren, seems to make a point of showing her defects right from the start.

The city is only two and a half miles from the mainland; we cross that gap by a double bridge that is so dull it might be leading to anywhere. Porters and guides hustle us towards the piers with such urgency that we feel the city may be about to sink beneath the waves, as we have been told it will one day. We see a gondola and make towards that. We ask the price for a ride through the city and Venice immediately teaches us a lesson about beauty; it is expensive. With a little bargaining, we manage to cut the price down to a smaller amount—but not by much. When we press harder, the gondolier, a man who looks romantic only on chocolate boxes, points us towards a large launch, which is the real urban transport of Venice. The launch is very noisy, it is very crowded, and it makes waves that are helping to undermine the city. We look back at the comfortable, quiet gondola, and realize that there is no point in trying to save money in Venice; the Venetians will never let you do it. We take the gondola.

The gondolier immediately becomes more gracious. It is not likely that he will sing nowadays, because he has been told so many times to shut up. To be sung to immediately after a long wait at an airport, a delayed train or a traffic jam on the highway is beyond human endurance. So the gondolier has learned to preserve silence, punctuated only by piercing shouts that seem to presage an immediate collision with another boat, but only mean "to the left", or "to the right".

That, unfortunately, is not the only noise. The water-buses have sirens, motor boats have klaxons, and outboard craft have deafening little motors. It may have been more attractive for Lord Byron; in his time there were no motors on the Grand Canal. But nowadays, in these first few minutes, with all the noise and confusion, we have the feeling that if it is a fairyland we have come to see, Walt Disney would have done it much better.

Then the Grand Canal turns a corner, and suddenly it seems as if Walt Disney had in fact had a hand in what we see. Indeed, had he been given the wealth that once poured into Venice, Venice might have been his immortal masterpiece. Palace after palace comes into view, each rising straight out of the rippling water, each with a delicate tracery of arches, some with lush little gardens, all with discreet balconies suitable for shy

By the last light of the sun and the first from the evening moon, a vaporetto, or water-bus, flashes up the Grand Canal. Beyond the domed Church of Santa Maria della Salute at right, cruise-ships—festooned with lights to celebrate their arrival in Venice—ride at anchor.

princesses to observe the world without being seen. A last and perfect touch are the tall poles jutting out of the water; they are placed there for boats to tie up to, and they are striped like barbers' poles.

The sight is so beautiful, so astonishing, that we forget the noise. We want the magic to go on and on, and never stop. Nor does it. We turn another bend and there are still more palaces. We glide under a pure white bridge that seems to have been drawn by some illuminator of medieval manuscripts, inventing his own city as he sat in his cell. It is all full of small arches, and it rises on either side to a small pavilion at the top. "The Rialto", says the gondolier; and we look back, feeling that all bridges should be white, and rise up on either side, and have a pavilion at the top. We begin to feel that Venice, after all, will not fail us.

The canal turns again. More palaces, with glimpses down other, smaller canals that run between them; some of these have miniature Rialtos riding across them. Ancient houses line their sides, with a profusion of flowers in their windows. Then, with the suddenness of a curtain rising in a theatre, we see a great sweep of buildings, each a place out of a legend. A tall tower—the one we saw before—lifts its pointed hat high into the sky. A cluster of domes nestles beneath it. And right at the waterside is the last and most astonishing of the palaces—that of the Doges, all pink tracery above, and, with arches below like lace. Nobody but the Venetians could have put together a panorama like this; nobody ever will again. And there, to complete the stupendous picture, once again is Santa Maria della Salute.

The gondolier ties up to an embankment, and with a magnificent gesture announces that he has brought us to the "Molo San Marco". St. Mark is the patron saint of the Venetians (after his death in Alexandria, the Venetians stole what is said to be his body by wrapping it up in pork so the Muslims would not discover it). Both this magnificent square and the church that dominates it are named after him. We settle with the gondolier, feeling that robbery is not a lost art in Venice, and we look about us.

There is a small piazza in front of us, adorned by two columns. We immediately wonder if that tall bell tower is on wheels; from the gondola it seemed to be in its logical place, hard by the Basilica of St. Mark, but now we see that it is on the other side of the street. Intrigued, we are drawn forward, and we come upon one of the world's most famous squares.

It has unfortunately acquired one of those 19th-Century clichés that never go away. St. Mark's Square is called "the drawing room". We do not have drawing rooms any more, and if we did, we would not allow them to be inhabited by tens of thousands of pigeons. But the name refers to more spacious days when the aristocracy of Europe and the rich of America lounged away their mornings and evenings in the cafés that line the square. The cafés are still there, and they are still for the rich: now one would need to be an oil sheik to do any prolonged lounging in them. The name of one of these cafés will raise an echo in the minds of readers of Victorian

For years the picture at right was accepted as a lucky photographer's authentic record of the fall of St. Mark's Campanile. Weakened by centuries of dampness and earthquakes, the tower shuddered and collapsed at 9.55 a.m. on July 14, 1902, leaving a gigantic heap of rubble (below). Now it is thought that the top photo may be more a product of Venetian acumen than fortuitous timing. Shutter speeds of the period probably were too slow to freeze the event so sharply, and there appear to be brush strokes in the dust cloud. The present tower was built as a replica of the fallen one.

novels: Florian's, with its orchestra, cropped up whenever 19th-Century authors wished to strike a note of dizzy elegance. Florian's is not elegant any more; and I, for one, am glad. I should not have enjoyed the creaking of stays and having to peer under those enormous hats that were *de rigueur* at Florian's in its days of glory. Denims are better.

One custom has survived, and that is feeding the pigeons. Inexplicably, fathers and mothers are convinced that their offspring never look more attractive than with birds sitting on their heads. Photographers abound; and so generations of visitors to Venice have writhed when, years later, a picture turns up showing them looking alarmed, silly and covered with pigeons against the stupendous background of St. Mark's.

Florian's, the photographers and even more the pigeons are all rather a pity. I think St. Mark's Square is best seen in the depth of winter, when on some days the wind-driven waters of the Adriatic flood it two or three feet deep. On such days Florian's packs away its tables and the pigeons roost and shiver on the roof-tops. The few people who venture abroad walk delicately along raised planks. Then, one is less distracted and can admire to its utmost the marvel of the architecture.

It confounds every principle of artistic good taste we have ever learned. Three sides of the square are pure Renaissance: arcades, columns, pilasters and friezes. There is even some Baroque cunning. The sides of the square look parallel, but they are not. They slope inwards, so that the square looks longer than it is, and our eyes are led to the basilica. But the basilica, forming the fourth wall, is a fantastic creation of the Byzantine style at its most oriental. It is lavish, it is complicated—and it is squat. There is no doubt about it: it is a very low cathedral. The correct thing would have been to give it a not very high bell tower. Instead the Venetians built a gigantic affair that soars 325 feet into the air. It looks as if, should it fall down, it would flatten the cathedral crouching below. In 1902 it did fall down, fortunately in another direction. The Venetians built it up again, lovingly, to its full height.

The basilica is built of coloured marble. The tower is built of plain dark red brick. It is stark in its lines, without a touch of fancy. And directly opposite it in the square is a gateway of pure nonsense. There is another tower over this gate, and halfway up in the tower is a statue of the Virgin Mary. In Ascension week, clockwork images of the Three Magi come out of trapdoors and bow to her. Higher up there is another show; this one goes on every day. Two giant bronze figures holding hammers strike the hours on a bell. To add to the interest, they are dressed in short goat-skin jackets that reach only to their waists, and are markedly naked below. Italian children (after being photographed with pigeons on their heads) always ask why, and Mamma replies that the men have left their trousers at home.

I fear my description may have been confusing; but it is accurate. The strange thing is that all this variety blends, and to perfection. The weather

The pigeons of St. Mark's Square, perhaps the world's best fed, may also be the greediest. This little girl prudently wears a hat and, when the birds demand more food from her plastic bag, she tugs the hat down for protection.

in Venice is not typically Italian. The summer sun is not golden, as it is in Rome. The winter skies are not pellucid, as they are in Florence. Venice has gales and lowering clouds, fog and rainstorms. But always, in any weather, the square is serenely perfect. It is not due to a sense of history: nothing of world-shaking importance ever happened here. It confounds all the teachings of all the professors of art, who are wary of writing about it. The only explanation I can offer, if it can be called one, is that when the Venetians were at their prime, they could do nothing wrong, even when what they did was plainly very wrong indeed.

A very good example of what I mean is right in front of us. I have said that the design of the square leads the eye to the basilica. Approaching the basilica more closely, we see four great bronze horses on a terrace over the main door. First, let me state what is wrong with these horses. The façade of the church is covered with statues and mosaics that are all clearly Christian, as is right and proper since this is a place of Christian worship. The horses are not Christian at all. They might, at a pinch, be thought to recall the Four Horsemen of the Apocalypse; but they have no riders. In historical fact their presence commemorates one of the most unchristian acts that has ever been committed.

At the beginning of the 13th Century, the Pope called for yet another Crusade (the fourth) to free the Holy Places from the Muslims. The response in men was satisfactory; the response in money was less so. The Venetians offered to finance the expedition, but they struck a typically Venetian bargain. The Crusaders had first to conquer certain Adriatic ports

Bride of the Adriatic

Venice lies in the north-west corner of the Adriatic on a collection of small islands that were originally little more than mud-banks intersected by tidal channels. From the shallow waters of the surrounding lagoon its domes and pinnacles rise, unforgettably, like a mirage. The main island, known in early times as the Rialto, is bisected by the curves of the Grand Canal and amounts to two-and-a-half square miles in area. It is crowded with the splendid edifices and monuments of its long history—most of them marked in the large-scale, diagrammatic map at right. The locations of other Venetian islands in the 22-mile-long lagoon are indicated on the small inset map below.

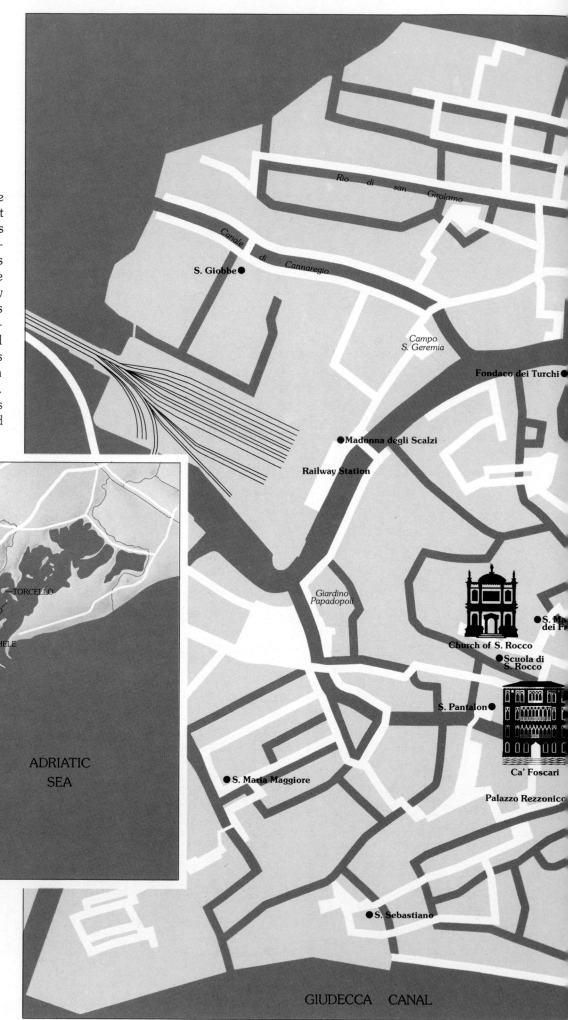

Cemetery

LAGUNA MORTA

Madonna dell'Orto

●**S. Maria dei Gesuiti**

●**S. Fosca**

Pesaro●

Ca' d'Oro

Fondaco dei Tedeschi

Statue of Bartolomeo Colleoni

Ss. Giovanni e Paolo

Rialto Bridge

Campo S. Polo

CANAL

GRAND

Arsenale

Torre del'Orologio

St. Mark's Square

The Campanile

St. Marks Basilica

S. Zaccaria

Riva *degli* *Schiavoni*

Procuratie Nuove ●*Molo* ●**Sansovino Library** **Palace of the Doges**
S. Marco

●**La Fenice Theatre**

●**Villa Barbaro**

●**Palazzo Dario**

●**Accademia**

S. Maria della Salute

S. Giorgio Maggiore

that the Venetians wanted for purposes of trade. The Crusaders obliged. They then went on to Constantinople, a most Christian city, and took it by storm, sacking and burning it very thoroughly. The Venetians, as bankers to the Crusade, demanded their share of the loot. Among it were those four horses. They were duly despatched to Venice.

They are made of bronze. They were once gilded, and some of the gold remains to this day. Nobody knows their origin, but they were made about the 3rd Century B.C., and may have been in Rome before they were carried off by Constantine to his new capital on the Bosphorus. They probably drew a chariot, and they are so superbly done that they might even have been created by the Greek sculptor, Lysippus.

Be that as it may, they have no place on a Christian church. When Napoleon conquered Venice he stole them anew, and when he got them to Paris he put them to proper use by setting them up on a triumphal arch. The Venetians could have done the same when the horses were brought back after Napoleon's fall. Instead they put them back in place, over the basilica door. It was a masterly idea. I have said that the cathedral is not high. The façade might well have looked a little small, a little inadequate. These four horses give it just that touch of monumentality it needed.

There is another example of this Venetian gift near at hand. A smaller square leads out of the big one, to the Molo San Marco. The view across the Grand Canal might be thought to be sufficiently picturesque by itself. Then again, it might lack dignity with its clutter of boats and masts. The Venetians therefore erected two enormous pillars towards the end of the square. One carries a bronze lion, the symbol of St. Mark, the other a statue of St. Theodore, a protector of the city. These columns are purely decorative; their purpose is to give the spectator something in the middle distance to hold his eye, before he goes on to look at the canal. They firm up the picture and give it strength. The Venetians planned with surpassing art.

But not all of the city. Going down the Grand Canal we saw smaller canals leading away from it, in a way that tempted us to explore. And that can be done from where we now stand looking at the bronze horses. We turn left, go under the nonsense tower with its two mechanical bell-ringers, walk a few yards, and we are immediately shocked.

There are no more palaces, no more ingenious perspectives. We find a muddle of little canals, narrow streets, crumbling bridges and, if it is summer, an overpowering bad smell. The canals (some little more than ditches) and the streets (few bigger than alleys) are lined with houses. By "lined" I mean the houses have no free walls and no space between them. Some are museum pieces dating back centuries; all are in a state of disrepair that no museum curator would permit. But they are lived in. Not willingly, by any means. The older Venetians stay on because they have nowhere else to go. The young move out to the mainland in search of light and air and proper sanitation.

A gondolier in traditional dress idles away his spare time—which in winter is most of each day—on a bridge over one of Venice's 177 canals. The brevity of their busy tourist season and the pressures of inflation cause the boatmen to demand frequent fare increases.

Our ancestors found all this romantic. Here and there in this warren one comes across a small square filled with market stalls heaped with fruit and vegetables. Our grandparents and our great-grandparents delighted in the sight and wrote prose about it that resembled the fruit. Now in the last quarter of the 20th Century, I suppose we can dimly discern what they meant. They were not as tired of heaped-up consumer goods as we are, since they had no daunting supermarkets.

But what did they do about the smell? In spite of relatively recent laws forbidding it, we can still see a window flung open and a shower of refuse emptied into the turgid waters, and even—a fine touch for the history buff —the contents of an occasional chamber-pot. I think our ancestors put up with this contamination because they themselves smelled worse than we do. They wore heavy clothing in all seasons; they bathed but rarely, and swam in the sea not at all unless under doctor's orders.

The canals twist and turn without any plan, and the alleys follow the same disordered pattern. At certain times of the day these alleys can be as crowded as a narrow city street at rush-hour. I suppose that there must be many like myself who dislike being jostled, bumped into and scraped by my fellow human beings. I can manage to dodge this experience even in the narrowest roads of Old Rome, having learned in many years nimble footwork and certain ballet-like twists of the body. Here, in what I shall call retro—or backstage—Venice, my art does not serve. I am frequently bounced like a ball on a pin-table.

Retro-Venice, in a word, is a slum. Two things, however, redeem it. At odd corners one comes across a church or a convent of great beauty. Once, when I was irremediably lost, I came suddenly upon a man on horseback high on a pedestal. This is the statue of a mercenary known as Colleoni. It is a masterpiece I have known from pictures since I was a child. Here, running across it when my head was turning from the bewildering tangle of streets and canals, I at last fully appreciated its full grandeur.

The other compensation is the Venetians themselves. They live in this insanitary warren with the greatest cheerfulness. We are used nowadays to discussing the mood of a city. In a slump, London is depressed, in a recession New Yorkers are on edge; Paris can be glum, gay, acidulous or indifferent according to the headlines in *Le Figaro*. Yet Venice, as I have known it over the years, has always been the same. The Venetians are rapacious on the Grand Canal; but behind it, they are reasonable among themselves. They do not talk much to visitors because to the ordinary Venetian, with his own distinctive dialect, even standard Italian presents some difficulties. But if you learn a little of their dialect they will tell you that they pride themselves on always getting by, whatever happens. They do not like gloom. They dispel it with jokes, often of an astonishing ribaldry. They drive hard bargains among themselves, but deep down they are loyal to other Venetians. Those who live in these dark and narrow houses are sad that the young, when they marry, go away. Venice, they tell you, may soon be half-empty, save for the tourists. They say this without any sentimentality. They would go themselves, if they could.

We shall need one of these Venetians if we are ever to find our way back to the Grand Canal. It does not help if we spot a landmark, such as a glimpse of the Campanile. Once again, it seems on wheels, and in a few moments we are more lost than ever.

Since visitors have been getting lost for centuries, the Venetians know how to handle the situation. There is no point in giving a stranger directions. Each alley, each canal and each bridge has its name, but pronounced in the Venetian way it is incomprehensible even to Italians born not an hour's distance away. So the Venetian goes with us, diving round corners, trotting across bridges and even apparently going right through private houses. At the first glimpse of either St. Mark's or the Grand Canal, he leaves us with a polite phrase. A Venetian expects to be paid for everything else he does for a visitor, but not for this.

We are back among the palaces. It would be reasonable to assume that this time they will look sham, as though we have been taken backstage, behind the scenery. We feel the very reverse. Once again the Venetians have been superbly right. They could have scattered these houses of the rich among the houses of the poor, as the Romans and Florentines did.. But Venice is much smaller than Florence or Rome. The effect would have been pretty, not grand. Gathering them together along the banks of this canal, they created the effect of magnificence—but in a purely Venetian way. This is the real reason why there is no city on earth like Venice.

In the beginning of this first exploration I supplied us with a private yacht. With renewed liberality I shall end it with a night in a palace. The Gritti is one of those on the canal. It was built in the 15th Century and it is perfectly restored. A fanciful arcade runs across its front, from which the original owners watched the passing pageant of the canal. The palace is now a hotel, and one of the most expensive in Italy. We take a suite, and find the furnishing much in the taste of the times when the palace was built, but infinitely more comfortable. It is, let us say, a summer evening. We hear music floating across the waters. A barge comes into view, gaily painted and lit with small lights. Round it, and following it as it makes its slow progress up the canal, are a score of gondolas and small craft. On the barge an orchestra is playing, and a man singing.

It is all very well done. But it is not, as we might think, an ancient Venetian custom. The songs, we notice, are not Venetian, but more often Neapolitan. It is a show put on for the visitor. The Venetians feel that we want something like this and, as ever, they are right. We do.

A City Awash

Even narrower than Venice's alleys are the duck boards spanning the floodwaters covering St. Mark's Square and posing a hazard to Venetians and tourists alike.

Venice, the city of canals, is a city of water, and never more so than when high tides and weather conditions combine to raise the sea level the few extra feet that carry it up on to the great St. Mark's Square. After the initial shock of the strange sight, there is an extravagant naturalness in the fact that the normally grey surface of the square should now consist of shifting aqueous light. The pattern of the submerged pavements appears magically sharp and fresh, and the surrounding buildings are reflected in the water with scarcely a ripple to distort them. But the beautiful vision has a grim side: because of changes in land and sea levels, floods are now much more common than a century ago. While the tourist may catch his breath at the uncanny charm of a city awash, the Venetians catch theirs with irritation at the inconvenience.

Umbrellas dot a raised catwalk that complements the geometry of pavements shining through floodwaters.

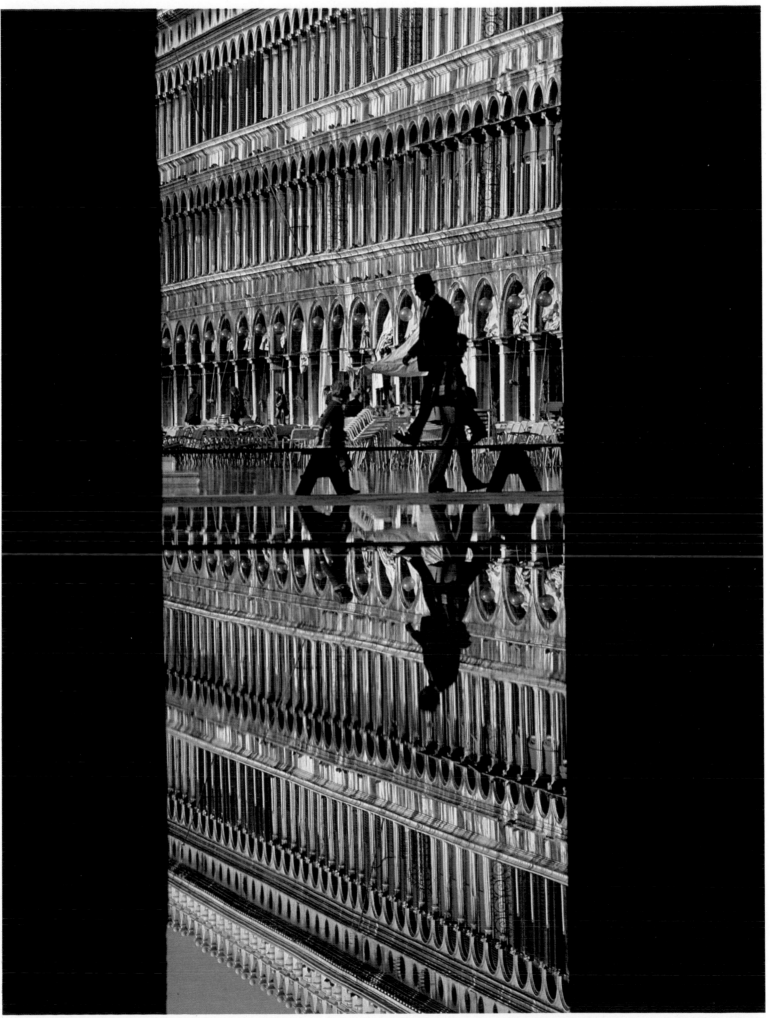

Reflections make a man on the catwalk seem to move between one façade below him and another above. Two other pedestrians scorn the safety of the catwalk.

In galoshes and a flapping black skirt, a Venetian woman sombrely surveys the flickering sheet of water that separates her from the far side of the broad square.

A bedraggled pigeon, unable to land on the pavement, prepares to wait out the flood on the back of a café chair.

In an interplay of levels, a fragmented reflection of the square's rosy buildings dances on the water's surface, while beneath it lies an abandoned moccasin.

At the foot of one of the banner-bearing flagpoles that stand before St. Mark's lies a battered emblem of today's beleaguered city—a collapsed umbrella.

As the water recedes, dry patches (at rear) begin to reappear on the square. With the sun shining and pigeons on the wing against the brightly lit, arcaded buildings, there is time to notice how strangely beautiful St. Mark's Square looks sheeted with rippling water—and devoid of the people who normally throng it.

2

Glorious Shadows of the Past

As the horizontal evening sun shines through the west doors of the Basilica of St. Mark's, the long shadows of a pair of visitors fall along the undulations of the ancient floor. The church, a storehouse of priceless religious art, stands adjacent to the Doges' Palace. Both edifices bear exceptional testimony to the wealth and power of Venice in its heyday.

Who were these extraordinary people who founded Venice? And why did they choose to build a city virtually on water?

They did so for the same reason we today make atom bombs: they were afraid. Originally they lived on the mainland in the territory we now call the Veneto. They were subjects of Rome. But Rome declined in power. The emperor moved to Constantinople. This move left a vacuum in Italy, and the barbarians from beyond the Alps moved in to fill it. The tribes were diverse—Huns, Visigoths, Lombards. Two of their leaders had names that even today are synonymous with terror: Alaric and Attila. Their military tactics were the same as ours. They killed everyone in sight, and then burned the place down.

On land the barbarians were irresistible. Indeed, by the 5th Century they had conquered a large part of Italy. But the people of the Veneto took note of the fact that the barbarians were clumsy in handling boats. So they abandoned their town and went to live on a cluster of islands off the shore. Water was not the only defence they had; there were sand-banks and shoals that grounded the boats of the barbarians and left them floundering about in the shallow lagoons. Thus by A.D. 452 (to accept the traditional date) a viable and defensible township was founded. It was later given the name of Venice.

The Venetians, as we can now call them, were left in peace. They multiplied, and soon there was no room for all of them on their little islands. They then took a bold step. Instead of sending their surplus population to the mainland (which would have meant abandoning them to the barbarians' mercy), they drove piles into the water and erected their houses on them. This had been done before. Back in prehistoric times, in northern Italy whole villages had been built on pilings out on lakes, for protection from wild beasts. But here it was done on a much bigger scale. Discovering that just underneath the islands' mud there was firm clay, the Venetians reinforced their pilings with layers of stone and planks, thereby creating blocks of land and narrow streets above the water level. The large island, which became Venice itself, was actually a pair of islands separated by the channel that now forms the Grand Canal. The Venetians shored up this channel and its innumerable tributaries and dredged them so they could be used as waterways. More and more buildings rose on the foundations anchored in the clay, and Venice became a sizeable community.

At first the Venetians ran their community in a thoroughly democratic fashion. They elected a council from among the leading personalities. But the members fell out among themselves. Factions arose and there was even fighting. The Venetians realized that a house divided against itself cannot stand, even when built on solid timber piles. They therefore chose one man to govern them, He was called the *duce*, or leader, as Mussolini was to be called centuries later. This name, in the Venetian dialect, became *doge*. From then on Venice was ruled—at least nominally—by doges until 1797, when Napoleon Bonaparte conquered Italy, dismissed the last Doge, and carried off the bronze horses to Paris.

The doges, with their magnificent robes and peculiar hats, have always struck the world as romantic and all-powerful. In fact, they were not much more romantic than the Lord Mayor of London, and like that functionary, wielded very little actual power.

One of the reasons the doges are thought to be romantic is that they lived in a legendary palace. It does not seem to be a building at all. I first saw it when I was 12 years old. To my child's eye it looked like a huge block of vanilla and strawberry ice-cream mounted on a base of sugar-icing. Then, of course, I knew nothing about architecture. I know a good deal more now, but it does not serve me much here. The palace being Venetian, it would be expected to break all the rules, and it does. Two sides match, two others do not. The two matching sides are perfectly symmetrical in all their hundred details—except for two windows that are quite out of line with the others. It is in the Gothic style. The Gothic architects were, elsewhere, serious men, bent on erecting solemn cathedrals. If, with the passage of years, I would no longer call it an ice-cream cake, I still feel that the Doges' Palace must be the world's most frivolous building.

But only in appearance. Its purpose was far from frivolous. It was built to be the headquarters of a tyrannous oligarchy that held the people of Venice under its thumb from the early Middle Ages down to the age of Napoleon. We have seen that Venice began as a democracy and went on to elect a leader. But as its merchants grew richer, the arrangement no longer suited them. The leaders of the big corporations today are inclined to think—or at least wish—that they are a law unto themselves; and they are never completely satisfied with any government unless they have it in their pockets. So it was with the merchants of Venice. They decided that since they were so successful in business, they were quite capable of running their city without kings, or parliaments, or votes. So they evolved a system by which all power was concentrated in the hands of a few families. The names of these families were written in a sort of social register called the "Golden Book". The chief members of these families were known as "The Worthy Ones"—a title that can express the feelings of a prosperous businessman about himself even today. But today there are laws to keep him in order. In Venice The Worthy Ones made the laws themselves. Like all top businessmen, they did not much like competition. It was next to impossible to join the select gang. The oligarchy did not

Among a multitude of finely sculpted angels, prophets and saints who crowd the ornate façade of St. Mark's, these humble water jug carriers supporting the basilica's gutter spouts go almost unnoticed. For all their practicality, they are still carefully rendered monuments to the artistic taste of the Venetians.

welcome new members, unless it positively had to. Beginning in 1297 with 1,200 families, the "Golden Book", in all the long centuries of its history, never rose above 1,600 names.

These Worthy Ones elected from among their members a board of directors known as the Great Council. When the Council proved too big to be wholly efficient, they chose from its members various executive committees always from the restricted circle of the "Golden Book". There had, of course, to be a chairman. This was the Doge. At first he had some power, but step by step, it was taken away from him, until in the end he had no political power at all. The less power he had, the more he was held in reverence. Everything was done in his name. Since Venice had ambassadors all over Europe, the legend grew of an all-powerful man who ruled his island city with the absolutism of an emperor of Byzantium. He was, indeed, surrounded by an almost Byzantine formality. But it was the merchants who ruled.

We are now to see if we can go inside the ice-cream cake and emerge with our wits about us. Without knowing a little of what the Palace of the Doges is all about, the visitor invariably emerges stunned. He walks gaping through a succession of vast rooms each more ornate and splendid than the one before. Gold shines everywhere, but especially on the huge carved ceilings, which swarm with figures. He sees walls covered with enormous paintings depicting legions of men, women, angels and cupids —until he reaches, in the end, the largest oil painting in the world. This opus, portraying Paradise, with a swarm of saints and angels adoring the Trinity, has so many figures in it that it takes some time to find out what it is all about. The palace's paintings glorify the deeds of the Venetians, which largely consisted, it would seem, of seizing other people's landed property by sending in their equivalent of the Marines.

Many of these paintings were done by great masters. Passing by them for the first time, one looks at them with awe; but I defy anyone to like them at this first glance. That takes time and study: and some knowledge of the trials and troubles of a creative artist working for a big commercial corporation also helps one's understanding. But even now, having seen the palace many times, I am sometimes struck by the idea that the principle behind these swarming compositions was the same as that of the producers of the "Folies-Bergère" in Paris—namely, to cram on the stage as many people as it will hold, and to show the maximum amount of bare flesh. Of this latter there must be at least an acre in the palace's paintings.

On a second visit the painted tumult and the riot of gold carvings begin to fall into a somewhat more orderly pattern. Going up a staircase called Golden (the walls are indeed covered with gilded stucco), we come to what we would expect—the private apartments of the Doge. They are comprehensible: some monarchs still live in surroundings like these. So can we, if we have a lot of money. It is the style of decoration preferred by

The city's bold guardian stands before a 16th-Century panorama of Venice.

Leonine Symbol of the City

St. Mark's winged lion—displaying the Latin text: "Peace be unto you Mark my evangelist"—appears almost as frequently in Venice as the gondola. When the Venetians adopted the Apostle as their patron saint they also accepted the beast associated with him. In 1516 the painter Carpaccio chose the lion as the subject for one of his last pictures (detail above) and modern designers have put it on ship funnels (top row, far right), paper decorations (bottom row, far right), and doorways (middle row, centre). Above a door of the Doges' Palace it shares honours with a doge (middle row, far right). It is also seen on a boat (top row, left), a clock tower (top row, centre), the Campanile (middle row, left), in a mosaic (bottom row, left) and among statues in a church (bottom row, centre).

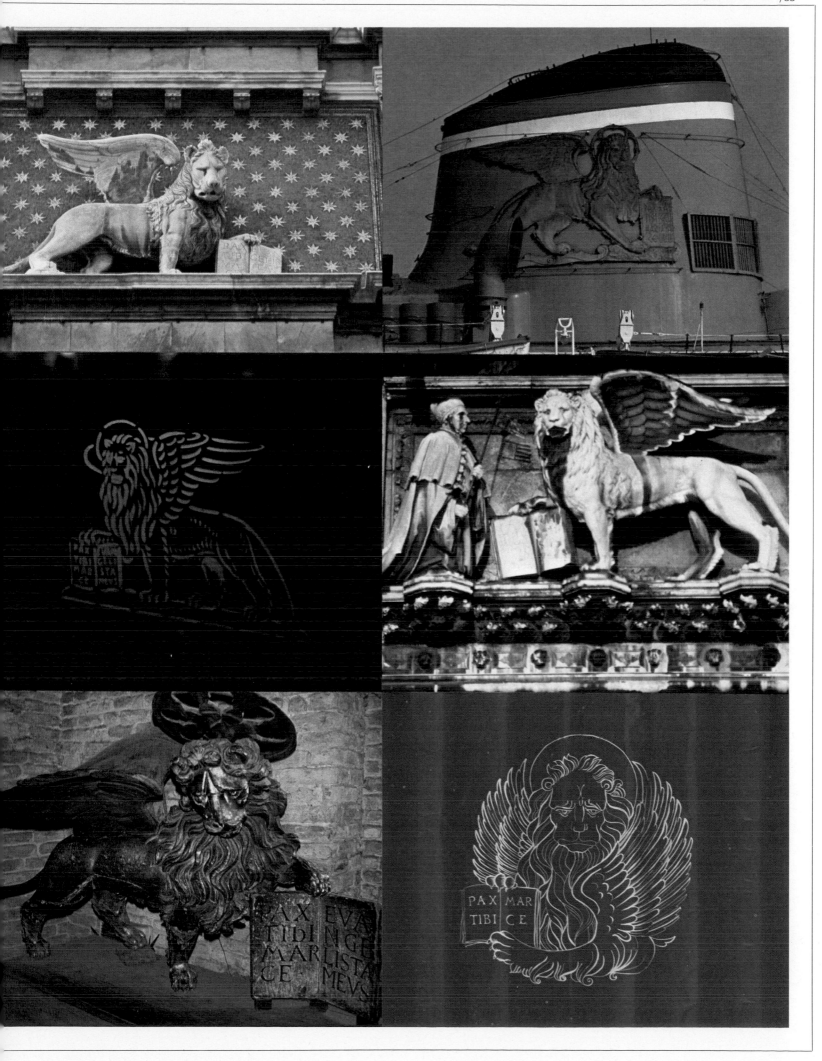

luxury hotels all over the world. The Doge's rooms present the original of that style, which, for want of a better name, I shall call Early Opulent. It is something of a relief to find a painting we can readily understand. It is in the Doge's private chapel: it is by the Venetian master Titian, and it shows the legend of St. Christopher carrying the Christ child across a river.

The second day at a very grand hotel is always better than the first. The heavy velvet curtains do draw properly; the gilded armchair actually can be used for sitting; the massive taps in the marble bathroom do provide hot water and not champagne. So it is with the Palace of the Doges. After our first visit, let us sleep on its splendours and go back the next day, this time with a plan on hand to find out what it is all about.

We stop in a vast hall. This, we read, is the Hall of the Great Council. Here, then, was where the Worthies gathered. We sit on the steps of the Doge's throne, which—and this is a clue—is remarkably austere; the ceiling is a riot of paintings and gilded carved wood. It is in this hall that the politics of Venice were conducted, and that fact may explain the ornate ceiling. Politicians make speeches, and most speeches become boring. Listeners, stifling a yawn, look up at the ceiling. This one must have been very consoling to the Doge's listeners. It said, unmistakably, that the Worthies were very rich. The late Aristotle Onassis was also very rich, but he needed his ocean-going yacht to remind everyone of the fact. This ceiling was the Venetians' yacht. We look again at the ceiling, and unless we are grimly egalitarian, we warm a little to the Worthies.

We pass on to another hall. It is the Hall of the Senate; one of those executive committees chosen from the Right People. The Hall of the Senate is, of course, opulent. As in the Hall of the Great Council, there is a rather bare place for the Doge. On the ceiling dozens of painted figures float about in the air—in a manner impossible for human beings until our own time when astronauts did it, also backed by huge sums of money. The subject of the painting (which is by another Venetian master, Tintoretto) is, inevitably, the "Triumph of Venice". Behind the Doge's throne is a painting by the same artist, showing a doge adoring the Dead Christ. Again, it puts the Doge in his place. He had to be a good Christian, on behalf of the Worthies who, business being business, might on occasion be less than good Christians themselves.

We pass on to the Hall of the Strong Box. Here was kept that Venetian equivalent of the Magna Carta and the Constitution of the United States: the "Golden Book". It must have been very fine to have one's name there: and yet being an oligarch has its difficulties. There are always awkward, ill-bred people who think that they are as good as you are. So, just beyond the Hall of the Strong Box we have the Hall of the Ten, a powerful committee that kept such people in order. Up above this hall is the Room of Torture. We can also, if we wish, cross a marble bridge that leads to the prisons. It is a pretty bridge with a pretty name: the Bridge of Sighs, so

Like a great ship cleaving the Adriatic mists, the Palace of the Doges—who until 1797 served as the titular rulers of the city republic—looms near the lagoon.

called because a prisoner crossing it might never see Venice again. Historians point out that this particular bridge was built after the tyranny of the Worthies had been much reduced, and that only one political prisoner is recorded to have passed over it. But the historians forget that there was a bridge there before this one.

How did the Worthies make all the money necessary to build and gild this place? The answer lies in a map of the world, but we must look at it with unprejudiced eyes. That, for us, is not easy. Nowadays the East is not our chief preoccupation. Such was not the case in the Middle Ages. Arabia, India, the "East Indies" and even China were the source of a European's luxuries. Silk for his clothes, spices for his food when it became tainted in the summer, jewels for his women, gold for himself—all Europeans quickly wanted these commodities. Before Vasco da Gama discovered the sea-route to India, such things had to be brought to Europe by land. From the time of the Roman Empire caravans crossed what is now Afghanistan and went on through Arabia up to Constantinople. From here their cargoes crossed Macedonia to the ports on the Adriatic, or were loaded on ships in the Levant.

Venice was the half-way point. Venetians were the middlemen; and, as we know, a shrewd middleman can grow very rich without having any particular talent. The Venetian merchants bought cheap and sold dear, as is the immemorial recipe for merchants. But some of them did have a talent, and that was for sailing ships. Being an island city helped. And so, for a time after the discovery of the sea-route to the East, Venetians continued to perform their auspicious function of middlemen. In the process they also became the finest navigators since the Phoenicians. The Phoenicians built Carthage on the profits of trade. Carthage has gone; and not a stone of it remains above ground. The Venetians built Venice; and it is still the glory and marvel of Western civilization. We owe the alphabet to the Phoenicians, because they needed it for their record keeping. We owe Venice to very similar businessmen who built it to show off.

It was another group of sailors who finally superseded the Venetians. Across Europe lies Portugal. The Portuguese had no gift for business, but they did have a gift for ship-handling. With the Venetians, a ship was an instrument for making money, or, in dire need, for making war. It was that and nothing else. For the Portuguese, a ship was an invitation to adventure. A remarkable man, Henry the Navigator, looked at the Atlantic, which beats so dramatically on Portugal's coast, and sent his seamen to find out what lay beyond the horizon. It was one of these adventurers who found the ocean trade route to India. Vasco da Gama stumbled across a meteorological fact that everybody on the shores of the Indian Ocean knew but had kept hidden from the Europeans (how, is one of the mysteries of history). This was that a wind called the monsoon blew in certain months of the year from the coasts of Africa to India. Catch that breeze, and all was plain

The 177-foot-long Hall of the Great Council within the Doges' Palace, where Venetian nobles once met to elect the republic's officers, is virtually an art gallery of Old Masters. The ceiling alone holds 15 major paintings, some of them important works by Veronese and Tintoretto, surrounded by 20 smaller works.

sailing. So Vasco found, and in due course, dropped anchor in Calicut, a town on India's west coast. The astonished inhabitants made up their minds to kill him, but he fled north and survived. He had not, of course, "discovered" India. But in the long run, it turned out that he had ruined Venice. Although at first he provided a great boon to the Venetian sailors and merchants, he had opened the way to India for the superior Portuguese navigators, and the fortunes of Venice slowly declined.

So far I have drawn a picture of the Venetians as commercially-minded people with a gift for art that sometimes, as in the Doges' Palace, led them to ostentation. This is true, but not the whole truth, for when the right moment came, these moneyed merchants were responsible, in a sense, for a rebirth of art in the form we have known ever since. I will try to explain how this came about.

Let us walk, in the mind's eye, around the business centre of any great city. One thing becomes obvious. Men with plenty of money follow the taste of their times. If it runs to classical columns and heavy pediments, these we shall have in every bank or insurance building. If it turns, as it does today, towards glass shoe-boxes set on end, there will be glass shoe-boxes. It happened that the Doges' Palace burned in 1483, 1574, and 1577. The façade survived, or was restored. The interior followed the taste of the times, and this varied with the times. But next to the palace is an example of what the Venetians could do with their money when taste was at its height: the Basilica of St. Mark, built between 1063 and 1073.

The style of the cathedral is not original. It comes from Byzantium across the sea, where the bronze horses were found. Now I am aware that the word "Byzantine" can produce, even in the most knowledgeable people, a mental numbness. It was so, for many years, with me. Then one day, irritated by my ignorance, I began to study the matter, making long journeys around the Mediterranean to do so. My irritation was so much like that felt by many people nowadays who deplore the fact that they know nothing about China except that the Chinese built a wall and made wildly expensive pots. So let me, before we go into St. Mark's, tell you something about the Byzantines.

They invented a style of art all of their own. They may have found a hint or two in Syria, when the Roman Empire transferred from Rome to the East. But that was not sufficient to raise such masterpieces as the church of St. Sophia in Constantinople, or to make the mosaics in Ravenna farther down the Adriatic coast from Venice. The inspiration was fresh, as full of life and originality as that of the Post-Impressionists in France.

The Western Christian notion of a cathedral is some soaring Gothic place that is intended to raise our thoughts towards heaven—or, in some cases, a great hall where thousands can gather to stare at some such awe-some figure as the Pope. The Byzantines thought quite differently. They had an awesome figure indeed: he was the emperor, who was regarded as being little short of God himself, He lived in his palace, attended by the most elaborate ceremonial, part of which consisted in his subjects prostrating themselves on the floor. Much of this was absurd—almost "Byzantine" as we say—but the Byzantines loved ceremony. In fact they loved it above all other things, except chariot-racing. So, when they came to build their churches, they made them into perfect settings for the ceremonies of religion. There were wide spaces through which gorgeous processions could wind. There were arches and corridors through which these processions could be glimpsed as they passed, thus adding greatly to the dramatic effect. Music is a major part of any ceremony, so they built domes in which the singing would solemnly re-echo.

At this point I would suggest you try to fit an upturned tea-cup on a square box much the same size. It is all very awkward, with gaps at the corners. The Byzantines solved this problem brilliantly. They made curved triangular pieces that joined the circular dome smoothly to the square building. These are called "pendentives".

The aim of a church was to teach the faith. The Byzantines agreed that this could be done better with pictures than with books, which people were too lazy to read, or with sermons during which they fell asleep. To make the pictures they chose mosaic, for two reasons. A mosaic is permanent, and it can be washed as easily as a pavement. (For these same reasons, all save one of the "paintings" in Rome's St. Peter's are mosaic.)

They next decided that the pictures should look real, but not realistic. That is to say, the Apostles, for instance, should be recognizable human beings, almost the faces you would meet in the street; but they should have some formal dignity that would raise them above the common herd and give them a touch of divinity. The idea plainly came from the emperor's court, where rigid formality gave him a divine aura.

With this information, we are ready to go into St. Mark's. Without it, in my experience, the church seems beautiful but alien. Clearly, we should choose an hour when there is some great ceremony unfolding. In recent years the Catholic church has tended towards starkness and simplicity in the principal rite, the mass. But not entirely. There still remains Pontifical High Mass, the most splendid ceremonial to be seen anywhere. Dozens of prelates and acolytes perform what has often been described as a sacred dance such as David performed before the Ark of the Covenant. Their movements centre around the splendidly robed bishop on his throne. Candles blaze, music thunders, the bishop changes mitres with the solemnity of a coronation, while the whole church smells of incense.

Such a ceremony then, is going on as we enter St. Mark's. Our immediate impression is that it is taking place in a vast box of gold. But this time the gold is not like that of the Palace of the Doges—it is not mere gilding. It seems to stream from the walls like some form of radiation. There is no need to sit primly on a chair to follow the proceedings. We do not need a

The five great Byzantine domes of St. Mark's Basilica took on their oriental appearance in the 13th Century when the outer covering of lead was added to the original squat brick cupolas. After the sack of Constantinople by the Venetians in 1204, an influx of Byzantine artists and looted treasures helped to turn St. Mark's into a spectacle of Eastern splendour.

prayer book. The people of Byzantium did not follow the liturgy: this they left to the priests. They went to church to behold a holy pageant.

We do the same. We climb a stairway that leads to a gallery that runs round most of the cathedral. This, in Byzantium, was meant for the women, who were segregated from the men. While the ceremony below runs its stately course, we see (for we are close against the walls, the gallery being narrow) that the golden glow comes from myriads of small pieces of coloured glass and stone, fixed side by side in mortar.

Against the gold background are hundreds of figures, robed in the Byzantine manner (and in Constantinople they were very dressy), telling the story of the Bible. Here Jesus enters Jerusalem, sitting on the ass, with the cloaks thrown down on the ground in his honour. There he sits in glory. On the pendentives of the dome are the four evangelists, staring at us with dark and thoughtful eyes. Behind them are portrayed houses, city walls, palaces all in a rather childish perspective.

This is as it should be, for these mosaics date from the childhood of Western art. As the clouds that had obscured men's minds and eyes in the Dark Ages began to roll away, the people of Italy began to look about them. The art of painting had been lost with the fall of the Roman Empire. We shall go on to tell of what happened to painting after that, but first I would like to pause, here in St. Mark's, to say why I have chosen to do so in Venice. The reason is that Venice is the best place in the world to do it. It takes time (and we shall take our time) and we must go step by step. But when the journey is over we shall have learned more about painting than

The gem-studded Pala d'Oro (Golden Screen) in St. Mark's Basilica consists of more than 80 panels surrounded by intricate goldwork. Although the screen was created in Venice, many of its delicately enamelled panels are Byzantine, probably taken from a monastery in Constantinople in the 13th Century.

we can learn in any other city. No matter how much we may feel we already know about art, unless we have been to Venice, we can never be sure that we know what we are talking about. That is why Venice has its special place in the history of our civilization. From cavemen onwards, there have been artists with the urge to draw and colour and, above all, convince the spectator that what he was seeing was in some way true to life. In the 13th and 14th Centuries that was especially true of Italy where, as now, there were striking faces to be seen on every street, and a clear light to see them by.

Four men began to paint—the four evangelists, as it were, of all the Western art that we have today. They were Cavallini, Cimabue, Giotto and later, Duccio. And the only examples they had to go by were mosaics like those we are looking at, here in St. Mark's, or at Ravenna, 90 miles down the coast. Yet these painters did not merely copy. A new spirit was abroad in Italy. Towns across the country had cleared out their dukes and marquises, and had set about ruling themselves. Human beings, quite ordinary ones, replaced the stiff figures of kings and princes as the centre of interest. So it was in art as well.

An artist must please his public or else he does not eat. The four whom I have called the evangelists were no exception. They humanized the Byzantine style, making step-by-step discoveries, blunders, and triumphs as they did so. One such triumph was Duccio's *Maesta*—"Madonna in Glory". The delighted citizens took it out from his studio in Siena in a joyous procession to the cathedral, where it can still be seen. They rejoiced because his Madonna was a real woman.

These mosaics in Venice that we are looking at as the Pontifical Mass proceeds below us are real in their own way, too. Their faces differ. One can imagine the artist getting his uncle to pose for St. Peter and his young assistant to stand in for St. John. Yet their attitudes are awkward. They would, you feel, crack if they moved.

We are so close up we can count the squares in the mosaic: we can watch the way the colours are blended; we can see the lines of the composition as clearly as if we were standing by the artist himself. But only after many visits does the greatness of the Byzantine style become clearer. That knowledge is an acquisition that gives a lifetime of new enjoyment—because we can now measure the achievement of Giotto, Cimabue and Duccio all the better by understanding what came before them. And what impresses us equally is that this vital contribution to art as we know it today was made possible through the largesse of Venetian businessmen—who, no doubt, scarcely knew what contribution they were making.

The ceremony is over. We go down from the gallery and, standing in an alcove, see the bishop conducted to the sacristy with magnificent pomp, giving his great ring to be kissed by the faithful as he passes among them.

It is now time to go to the keystone of our understanding of Venice: the Pala d'Oro, the front-piece for an altar. Once it was used to cover the main altar of the cathedral, on the great feast days of the church, but now it is too fragile and too precious to be moved from its place in the sacristy.

It is approximately three and a half metres long and one and a half metres high. It bedazzles with gold, jewels and pictures on enamel. I would like to state what it is worth, for that is a very human question to ask in Venice; but it is beyond all estimation. Way back in 1796, when the Venetians rose against the rule of the doges, someone took an inventory of what treasures the Pala d'Oro contained. Let the list speak for itself: 1,300 pearls, 400 garnets, 300 sapphires, 300 emeralds, 90 amethysts, 90 rubies, four topazes, two antique cameos and no fewer than 80 pictures in finely wrought enamel.

Most of these pictures were loot from Byzantium. There are even two panels showing the emperor and empress of that city, although the emperor has been re-worked into a portrait of a doge. In one sense, then, this scintillating marvel is not Venetian. In another, it is; for it was an Italian goldsmith, working in Venice, with the Doge's money and the city's treasure, who in 1342 put the whole thing together. His name was Gian Paolo Buoninsegna. And in his brilliant work of art he assembled a monument to the essence of Venice, a city midway between Europe and the wealth, the jewels, the skills of the East. For these precious stones came, by way of Byzantium, from distant India to enrich the culture of the West.

Treasure House of Colour

A 700-year-old mosaic above one of the doors of the Basilica of St. Mark shows the church with the four bronze horses that are still in place there today.

For the nine centuries since the consecration of the present church the Basilica of St. Mark has been the central symbol of Venice, proudly embellished from age to age as the showpiece of the city's prosperity. Progressively enriched both inside and out, it burgeoned from a relatively plain but stately structure— shown above in the earliest known representation—into a uniquely rich work of art that has challenged the descriptive powers of generations of visitors. The following pages make no attempt to give a full account of the artistic riches of St. Mark's, but only to record some of its smouldering effects of light and shadow, and to give a hint of what the American novelist Henry James—whose evocation of the interior is among the most successful—called "the molten colour that drops from the hollow vaults and thickens the air with its richness".

Light gleams off the gilded mosaics that cover the massive piers and lofty cupolas inside St. Mark's (above). The present building, begun in the 11th Century to replace an earlier church, preserves a strongly Byzantine character overlaid by Venetian extravagance.

Ninety-three feet above the floor, mosaic-lined cupolas (left) glow like inverted wells of golden light. The mosaics in the central cupola were executed in the 13th Century; the 12th-Century design in the cupola over the nave (far left) represents the Apostles at Pentecost.

Evening sun striking through the basilica's west windows ignites the mosaics clothing the vaulted piers into an incandescent blaze of gold, and turns the 17th-Century figures of Christ and an angel into contrasting black silhouettes. The gilded pieces making up the mosaics are set at slightly different angles so they will catch and reflect all available light.

Beside the great Gothic wheel of the rose window (above), set in place in the 15th Century, a single shaft of light picks out one sensitively modelled face from a mosaic scene on the wall. Together the mosaics inside St. Mark's cover the astonishing area of about one acre.

A broad stripe of sunlight lies across the exquisitely complicated floor of marble mosaic, as intricate as a finely worked carpet. Against a wall lined with tall marble panels of richly variegated colour patterns, a priest sits waiting in his confessional.

Crammed with intricate and detailed scenes illustrating the Creation and the story of Adam and Eve, this small cupola in the atrium, or entrance hall, of the basilica contains some of the liveliest and most natural mosaics of the Venetian school. Executed in the 13th Century, after an earlier Byzantine design, they are among the best preserved of the original decorations in St. Mark's.

Touches of gold glow among the dark colours and solemn faces of the eloquently gesturing worshippers in this 13th-Century mosaic in the south transept.

3

A Flair for the Theatrical

What of the ordinary Venetian—the poor man, the tradesman, the butcher and baker, and candlestick maker for those altars in St. Mark's? Did they really knuckle their forelocks for those worthy families?

Walking beside the little canals in backstage Venice, buying things from the stalls in the squares, I find it difficult to believe that they ever did. Italians do not change that much. Romans still make sarcastic jokes about the Pope, as they have for centuries. They still love to make indecent remarks about passing foreigners (especially female) in their incomprehensible dialect, and with a flashing smile as if they had paid a compliment; it is a game they have played since the very first Holy Year in 1300 when Rome was nearly bursting with pilgrims. Neapolitans still use vast cunning in evading authority, a craft they learned under a succession of foreign masters; and the Florentines still look and act like those elegant portraits hanging on the walls of their galleries.

The Venetian is no exception to this rule, He has not changed and he certainly is not humble. He stares you straight in the eye, whoever you are. If you are rude he will give you as good as you send, with all the verve and wit of the London Cockney. It is still possible to see a well-heeled Venetian arguing with his servant, and getting much the worst of it.

It happens that we have a perfect picture of the bourgeoisie of Venice when the city was in its glory. To see it, we must go to a play. I shall have to invent the performance, however. The plays you see in Venice today are most likely to be solemn works of social significance, because they are the only ones to get government subsidies. Not the one I have in mind. The play we are going to attend was written by Carlo Goldoni in 1760, and it is a comic masterpiece.

We go to La Fenice. It is an 18th-Century theatre, built some years after the first night of Goldoni's play but the only surviving example of the dozen theatres that flourished in his time—the Venetians were passionate theatregoers. (Nowadays they are passionate goers to the football game, preferably at home in front of the television.)

La Fenice is highly ornate, in the manner of the Palace of the Doges— and even more so today because what we see is not the original theatre (which burned down) but a mid-19th Century restoration. In taste it can be faulted, but I do not object. All the gold, the plush, the chandeliers and the row upon row of boxes give me the impression that I am once more being taken as a child to that improbable, astonishing and unforgettable world— the *theatre*. Today, when I go to a modern theatre, functionally designed

A Venetian citizen, squinting out across the water, conveys some of the traditional attributes of his fellow inhabitants. He appears to be shrewd and self-reliant, and there is a touch of flamboyance about his hat and tie. Yet, in this threatened city, his cocky face also seems to betray a trace of anxiety, perhaps even melancholy, over the future.

and with nothing extravagant except the price of the ticket, I see better, hear better, and forget the show sooner. La Fenice gives you a sense of childhood treat as soon as you sit down in your box.

It is just this sense of occasion that delighted the Venetians: in fact they spent most of their leisure time thinking up occasions—masked balls, fêtes on the Grand Canal, banquets where everybody dressed magnificently—and, above all, the theatre. Unfortunately, or perhaps fortunately, as it turned out, there were no good plays until Carlo Goldoni came on the scene. The English had their Shakespeare and Jonson and Marlowe to show them how human and exciting the theatre could be. Italy had produced no such geniuses. Its playwrights were serious-minded intellectuals who were bent on showing the audience their knowledge of the Latin and Greek classics, just as today Italian playwrights of the younger generation are anxious to show how well they understand Karl Marx.

Then there burst upon the scene in Venice an entirely new form of entertainment. It had nothing to do with playwrights, or even the written word. It sprang up first among the actors themselves, tired as they were with spouting stilted poetry. It was called the Commedia dell'Arte and it prepared the ground for Goldoni. I should explain at once that the last word in that name does not mean "Art"—quite the contrary. It means "profession", "craft", "skill", as a carpenter is skilled. It was the actors, the ordinary ones, showing what they could do.

They formed touring companies, of which the most famous were those of Venice; and they delighted all Europe. They scrapped the formal texts, or "lines", as we would say. The director (who was also an actor) wrote a "scenario". This word has had an unfortunate history since then, first in film-studios and then descending to its use by generals and politicians. Originally the scenario was just a large sheet of paper on which was written the barest outlines of a plot; and those plots were taken not from the classics but from the daily life of the Venetians.

The director distributed the parts (casting, in Italy, is still called "*la distribuzione*"); soon each actor knew pretty well what part he or she would get, since they specialized. There was a set of stock characters. The principal one was a typical Venetian merchant—old, shrewd, but good-hearted when it came to the pinch. He played in a mask that covered the top of his face, a convenient device because most of the actors were young. Generally the scenario called for him to have a daughter on whom he doted but who betrayed him in some way with a lover. The name of this merchant was Pantalone, and Shakespeare lifted him bodily when he drew his portrait of Shylock in "The Merchant of Venice". The second character was the Doctor, who also wore a mask. He was a pompous know-it-all with an answer for everything (invariably absurd) who spoke in an elaborate language, often pure nonsense, such as is used by some of our lesser sociologists today. Two other masked characters were the "*zanni*". Both

The grim mask above represents one of Venice's best-loved theatre characters, the role of a wry old man named Pantalone, whose invention dates back more than four centuries. This mask was worn by young actors in Commedia dell'Arte troupes who played the part in the 1700s. The jolly face on the statue at right belongs to the popular 18th-Century comedy playwright Carlo Goldoni, who made Pantalone a standard character in many of his works.

were servants, one called Arlecchino, and the other Brighella. Arlecchino wore a tattered costume, the rents and tears of which eventually were covered by coloured patches; those were the patches that Picasso immortalized in his pictures of Harlequin.

Four lovers, without masks, completed the troupe, Florindo and Lelio (the last often the son of the Doctor) and Rosina and Rosaura. While the masked characters spoke in the Venetian dialect, the lovers used a purer Italian. The reason for this is that Italian is a beautiful-sounding language, but Venetian is the very reverse—and better for low humour.

These actors studied the scenario and then made up their own lines. Nothing was written down. What they said varied with their moods or that of the audience. The performance always went at a tremendous pace and called for immense skill on the part of the actors. This skill they polished to such a high degree that people marvelled wherever they went. One company settled in London. The date was 1577, and one of the marvellers was Shakespeare, who in addition to Pantalone, borrowed their invention of the *zanni* for his Fool. Another company, this one in Paris, had no less a pupil than Molière.

At home, however, in Venice, the Commedia dell'Arte was becoming too successful. The audience, delighted at seeing their neighbours depicted on stage (no one, I think, ever sees himself when he goes to a comedy), roared with laughter at the actors' quips. It is a temptation of course to the finest comic actor, when he raises laughs, to want to raise more next time. There were, by definition, none of the hack gag-writers of which we have so many today—and in time the actors' inspiration ran thin. They took refuge, like a failing stand-up comedian, in broader and broader sex jokes. The Venetian's sense of humour runs to considerable coarseness. Their jokes, when told in a gondola, are funny, but they could not appear in cold print, even in our day. For a while, the Commedia dell'Arte held its audience; but it was beginning to be clear that something new was wanted. What?

Living in the Palazzo Cent'Anni in Venice was an 11-year-old boy who, in the manner of 11-year-old boys, decided that he knew the answer. But this one wrote a comedy that had all the verve and actuality of the Commedia dell'Arte—and one in which the actors had to learn their lines. His father was impressed, not only by the play, but by the fact that he had a problem on his hands. The father was a distinguished physician, and the theatre was no place for a son of his. So young Carlo Goldoni was packed off to the Jesuits, to be taught to be serious.

But when he was 14, Carlo ran away. He smuggled himself aboard a boat that carried a company of strolling players, and he was immediately enchanted with their carefree way of life. He liked the gaiety, the confusion, the noise, the jokes—and the girls. His autobiography is eloquent on the episode, and it leaves a modern reader in little doubt when he had his first affair. All his life he was a charmer.

All his life, too, he had a conflict. While he was head over heels in love with theatre, he had moments when he saw its tawdriness and sham. He adored actors, but knew their falsity. (The girl he eventually married was not an actress.) Goldoni was essentially a writer of prose, and many other writers have had the same division in their thoughts. The American Henry James is an outstanding example. He was hell-bent on success in the theatre; but after a disastrous first night he would bombard his friends with letters saying how happy he was to be returning to his real profession, that of writing novels.

Novels as Henry James knew them had not been invented when Goldoni was a boy. And in any case, the young man was forced to accept his father's plans for him and study law. At college he wrote an uproariously funny play about his fellow students and his teachers, for which he was promptly kicked out. He returned to Venice, where he did finally get his law degree but, as often happens, few clients. He ran into debt. He joined another group of players and wrote scenarios for them, this time for money. But when he tried to persuade them to learn lines they flatly refused. Meanwhile, his scenarios were a hit.

All the same, he returned to practising law, as became his double character, and he continued in this profession until he was 40. Then quite literally, life began for him, as he tells us in his autobiography.

He had written a scenario for a company of players in Venice. But this time he had reverted to his earlier ways and had written out the dialogue for the actors. The company, looking for something new to hold the public's interest, gave up their professional prejudices and tried out the idea. With the Venetians, the play, called "*The Clever Woman*", was what we would today call a smash hit. They clamoured for more.

There was only one person who could give them that, and it was Goldoni. A competing company sent their Pantalone to him, bearing an offer to make him their permanent writer of scenarios, dialogue and all. The respectable lawyer in Goldoni turned down the offer at once. He had finally begun to prosper in the law as well, and he was understandably reluctant now to give it up. But Pantalone pleaded, wheedled, begged and enticed, with all the gestures and comic grimaces he had learned in his trade. Still Goldoni resisted. Pantalone redoubled his efforts. He put on a star performance for an audience of one, and soon he had his audience rolling in the aisles. Before Goldoni could recover himself, Pantalone in a grand gesture threw some gold coins on the table, and Goldoni was lost and found: lost to the law, found by the Venetian theatre. He was to become one of Venice's most famous sons.

So: We are, let us say, Venetians—not too young, not too old, not too rich (we do not belong to the Worthy Sixteen Hundred) and yet again, not too poor. We have enough money to own a private gondola and maintain the gondolier, his wife and innumerable children. (I say innumerable

Venice was built for an age of slim gondolas and people on foot. The only passages that are narrower than some of the minor canals (right) are a number of cramped back streets such as Calle della Malvasia (far right), down which two landbound gondoliers prepare to thread their way.

Before the curtain rises, house lights bathe the interior of La Fenice, Venice's most beautiful and important theatre, with a feeling of warmth and intimacy. The 18th-Century building was reconstructed after a fire in 1836. In spite of the space lavished on rising tiers of private boxes, the theatre seats 1,500 people.

because we have never been able to keep track of them as they arrive year by year. But we understand why our gondolier is not dismayed by this: after all, he wants to be sure he will have gondolier sons to look after him when the chill winter fogs of the canals have eaten into his bones.)

We turn off the Grand Canal and go up a narrower one. The evening damp begins to make our own bones shiver, so we draw our great heavy capes about us. Romantic as these capes look in the paintings of the time, they were as utilitarian as an umbrella in London.

We pull up at the theatre. There is a confusion of gondolas, tying up to those posts shaped and coloured like barbers' poles. Lights gleam on the water. There is a flash of cloaks as the audience steps ashore. While we wait to tie up, we admire the scene. We, as true Venetians, will never tire of admiring the scene. If we have a guest with us (a "foreigner", say, from Milan), we will point out how beautiful the scene is several times; and he, if he is wise, will agree several times too, He has been warned about the Venetians' overwhelming pride in their city. The foyer is ablaze with candles and the uniforms of an army of flunkeys who dispose of our cloaks. An attendant even more magnificently uniformed than the flunkeys conducts us with great state to our private box. Arrived at the door, we hand him the keys; and with a flourish and a bow, he lets us in.

We are late arrivals. The theatre is almost full and the noise is deafening. If we wish to say anything to each other we shall have to shout to be heard above the roar of conversation. Venetians, in any form of entertainment, get the thing going by all talking at once. They will also talk through a concert, not quite so loudly but enough to make the musicians scrape away as hard as they can go, and the singers to yell.

Great chandeliers illuminate the theatre; the candles will burn throughout the performance. This is quite proper. The magnificently dressed audience are quite as much part of the show as the actors, and they have spent a lot of money on themselves in order to be seen.

The curtain rises; that is, it is hauled up in two halves. We consult a programme, which consists of a single sheet of paper, and we see that the play is called "The Superior Residence". The residence is depicted on canvas flats, but they are painted with such extraordinary tricks of perspective that we are sure we see mirrors with carved frames, pictures, windows and even ornate consoles. It is a very superior residence indeed.

Workmen are making alterations under the urgent direction of Oswaldo, their boss. They run up and down, fall off ladders, upset buckets and trip over one another. These antics are designed to fill in time until we, the Venetians, are willing to stop our gossiping, which we are reluctant to do. Besides, the knowing among us have something to tell the others: Goldoni himself has taken a new house, and we all know what a trial that can be. The palaces on the Grand Canal are like the scenery on the stage; they are designed to be seen from the front only. Inside they are planned— if planned at all—without any consideration for the comfort and convenience of the tenants. We expect Goldoni to make fun of this. We, meantime, enjoy the knock-about at the beginning of the play, perhaps with a little nostalgia. The actors of the old Commedia dell'Arte were superb clowns. A pert maidservant comes on; she rebukes Oswaldo for dawdling, swears she is not one to gossip, then tells everything. We delight in this. We Venetians always pretend to be immensely discreet, but are the most inquisitive, nosy tittle-tattlers in all Italy, and we are wryly proud of the fact.

The grand house has been bought by the maid's employer, Anzoletto, for much more than it is worth and much more than he has got, He has done this to please his new wife, a pretentious woman who gives herself the airs of a great lady, but—and the maidservant throws her lines at the audience—has brought him not a penny as her dowry. We laugh. We settle down for a good time. The play will be about either love or money, and we much appreciate both.

Now Anzoletto's sister storms in. She is enraged. The new wife has put her in a back room. We all know that the majority of the rooms in a Venetian palace are back rooms; nobody above the servant class wants to live in them, lightless, airless and gloomy as they are. So there is a perennial battle for those rooms fronting on the canal.

And Anzoletto does not know what to do about it. That becomes clear the moment he is on the stage. He has no mind of his own. He follows the

This painting by Gian Domenico Tiepolo (1727-1804) perfectly captures the licentious frivolity of Venice's protracted pre-Lenten carnival in the 18th Century.

advice of the last person who talks to him. He has altered the arrangement of the rooms half a dozen times. One such adviser—who is with him now—holds up his hands in horror to hear that Anzoletto has placed the master bedrooms on the *north* side. Impossible! He and his wife will freeze to death in winter. This appeals to us all. Cold and damp are the plague of Venice during its by no means short winter, and the bigger your house, the worse you suffer from it. It is the penalty for building a fairy town on water.

Anzoletto immediately gives orders for the great bed to be brought into the reception room and for all the other plans to be changed—which later will give us an opportunity to see some more knock-about. But just now we are absorbed in another incident drawn from our daily lives. Oswaldo, the workmen's boss, threatens to call his men out on strike if he is not paid. Drawing himself up, Anzoletto tells Oswaldo to remember he is dealing with "a man of honour". Oswaldo ducks his head humbly but turns to the audience: with one of the superb sneers that came from the Commedia dell'Arte, he says, "A man of *honour*". This does not perhaps please everybody in the boxes (who quite probably have found themselves in poor Anzoletto's situation); but a howl of joy goes up from the audience downstairs, where the seats are cheaper, and particularly from the playgoers right at the back, where they stand for nothing.

Now the young wife sweeps on to the stage. She is accompanied by a very aristocratic gentleman, whom she constantly informs that she has been brought up most genteelly and is used only to the finest things. But here I shall not vie with Goldoni. This is how he captures the pretensions of the social climbing wife (her name is Cecilia): he has her speak to a woman friend about going to the theatre. The friend says, "When my husband is in Venice we go to the Opera or to see a comedy once or twice a week. But as he is not here at the moment, I stay at home." To which Cecilia grandly replies, "If you would care to use one of my boxes, *do* let me know and I will let you have the keys. I have a box at all the theatres you know. And please do borrow my gondola." Her friend protests. She really does not go out when her husband is not in Venice. We approve of this statement. Venetian ladies are supposed to be modest, chaste and retiring. When not accompanied by their husbands, they appear in public only on the terraces of their palaces. Cecilia, however, has heard of the latest fashion among the upper crust. She says: "When your husband is here, do you always want him with you?" Her friend says she does, and Cecilia is in full flood: "How embarrassing for the poor man! One should have a little pity on one's husband, I always think. Let him do what he wants and go where he wants, that's what I say. I mean to say—if one can't even go to the theatre without one's husband—well, what *can* one do."

This produces great joy in boxes and ground floor alike. Goldoni has made a neat stab at a Venetian custom of which we are sometimes a little ashamed but which, mostly, amuses us—the *cicisbeo*. This is a man who dances attendance on a high-born lady—a wife, say, of The Worthy Ones. She has to maintain her respectability. So she chooses from a suitable admirer a person to go out with her, help her into her gondola, dance with her at balls and pick up her fan when she drops it. Her husband, usually being away from home making money, does not mind. He ranks the *cicisbeo* as something that goes with his fleet of gondolas and his 50 servants. At least, the *cicisbeo* saves him from sitting through fashionable but interminable operas. And whether or not the *cicisbeo* is his wife's attendant or her lover as well depends on the husband.

The first act is over. We leave our boxes for small rooms where refreshments are served. Friends from other boxes come in, and we note that more than one high-born lady has her *cicisbeo*. We treat him with the same elaborate courtesy as we would treat a woman. We do not pity him. We are quietly proud of Venice's reputation of being a wicked city. Not only our *cicisbei* but our elegant courtesans are the envy of the rest of Italy. And the rest of Italy comes to enjoy our Venetian beauties, bringing a lot of money and leaving a lot of it behind.

Act Two begins and, as we expect, Anzoletto gets what was coming to him. His creditors descend on him like a pack of wolves, strip him of his possessions and seal his old home, leaving him penniless in his new residence. His ambitious wife turns on him in a fury and, with a vulgar touch or two, makes it plain she is no lady at all. Hearing the bad news, her aristocratic friends, with an infinitude of courtesies, desert her. Who is going to save the situation? There is nobody with money in sight. Off-stage, indeed, is an uncle of Anzoletto—rich enough, but he will not do; he made his money selling meat. Naturally, the new wife will have nothing to do with so vulgar a person; and, besides, uncle has quarrelled with his nephew.

Act Three and here he is: old, crotchety, sharp-tongued, yet with a kind heart that he endeavours to conceal. He is Pantalone. And his lines are superb. Here they are, without, unfortunately, the rich Italian voice, the gruff slurring of the Venetian speech or the sweeping, expressive Venetian gestures, which can express utter contempt with an elbow. Uncle has been asked to help. He replies:

"I know all about it. You think I don't, eh? Let me tell you there's nothing I don't know about those two. I know her brother's in debt up to his eyes. I know that in two years my nephew's got through ten thousand ducats running after that precious wife of his. She's the one who's ruined him. He had no time for me any more. Couldn't even come and see me. If he saw me in the street he'd go out of his way to avoid me. I wasn't well enough dressed for him. I didn't wear lace on my cuffs. Oh, I know it all. I even know what that trumped-up aristocrat of a strumpet of his says about me. I upset her stomach! I'm a disgrace to her! She couldn't bear to call me uncle! Let her wait till I call her my niece! That'll be the day! The little shrew! Scum! Riff-raff! That's all she is!"

The whole theatre bursts into applause. We love long speeches (what Italian does not?), but they are usually empty of everything but wind. We applaud this one for its sentiments. The audience in the cheap seats applaud because we are Venetians and there is a tradesman in every family's ancestry. The Worthy People in their boxes applaud as well, because that upstart of a wife is getting the drubbing she deserves. We think it is a pity that Goldoni has given his best actress so unsympathetic a part. In his previous plays she brought tears to our eyes.

As if our own genius, our own Venetian Goldoni, hadn't known that all along! For now here she is, the snobbish, wilful, extravagant young wife who has ruined her husband—kneeling at Uncle's feet and admitting she is wrong. She is confessing that she has always been a spoiled brat. She takes the blame for the ruin of her husband. "Everybody is mocking us", she says. "Everybody is scorning and despising us. Tomorrow morning we shall be on the streets. But", she says, and she makes us hold our breath by a gesture, "who *is* my husband? He is your nephew, and I am your niece."

There is a lump in our throat; she has touched our hearts. The family, rich or poor, is the life-blood of Venice. She is the Prodigal Daughter-in-law, pleading to be welcomed back.

Pantalone responds: "Make out a list of your debts and I'll do what my heart tells me to do—and which you don't deserve, you worthless young good-for-nothing."

There are five more minutes of the play, but we are already adjusting our stocks, brushing our hats and shifting our lace trimmings. It has been a long play, and we wonder if our gondolier has got drunk, as he usually does.

Fortunately, he is sober and bursting with gossip. We know he has a pretty young mistress among the players, so we ask him if he knows who were the originals of Goldoni's characters. They are so lifelike, there must be some. He knows the names of all of them, and entertains us with a lot of scandal that Goldoni was content only to hint at.

We have been invited to a supper. Our gondolier takes us to a landing stage. Footmen holding torches line its sides. We give our gondolier a ducat to buy himself and his friends a drink, and go into the palazzo. More footmen line the entrance hall, this time holding candelabra. There are even two Negro pages. We walk through the rooms. It is, we whisper to each other, a very Superior Residence, and we wonder (such is the wickedness of Goldoni) whether our host can really afford it.

Regal Day on the Grand Canal

A caorlina, a boat originally used for carrying food supplies, surges past watchers resting on a float, in one of the regatta's heated competitions.

Leaning into their oars with a vigour that dispels any image of Venice as a tired museum city, crew members of a *caorlina* (above) desperately try to overtake a rival boat in one of the races of the *Regata Storica*—"historical regatta"—Venice's great annual water festival. On the first Sunday in September, Venetians (many in lavish Renaissance costume) and visitors throng the banks of the Grand Canal, which for the occasion are festooned with brilliantly coloured banners, velvet drapes and damask hangings. After a parade down the Grand Canal by lavishly decorated boats come the eagerly awaited races, rowed between crews from different districts of Venice in their two-oared *gondolini* and six-man *caorline*. The whole day is a stunning show, rich in props and pageantry—a spectacle that the Venetians, with their flare for the theatrical, dearly love.

These bissone, put to use only once a year in the regatta, are manned by gondoliers in 15th-Century costumes.

Stately Parade from the Past

The origins of the 700-year-old regatta are shadowy. One story suggests that it began with a grimly earnest pursuit of raiders who had kidnapped some Venetian women. But the grand procession of today's regatta re-enacts a later event: a spectacular welcome to the visiting Queen of Cyprus in 1489. The ceremonial boats, heavy with carved figures, are reminders of the great era when Venice was known as *La Serenissima*—"the most serene".

Leading the flotilla of gondolas down the Grand Canal comes an elaborate ceremonial bissona, loaded with gilded carvings and rowed by 18 crewmen.

Underlining Venice's maritime character, statues of Neptune appear on the bissone above and at right.

Symbol of an Opulent Age

The elegantly appointed boats called *bissone* are modern reproductions, but their ornate designs—heraldic crests of noble Venetian families, and figures of allegorical subjects— date from the age when Venice was a rich sea power. The *bissone* are stored in the *Arsenale*, the shipyard that, in the heyday of the city's power, spread the word "arsenal" through the world. Here, it was boasted, a complete galley could be built and fitted out in a day.

With a bunch of gladioli in his fist, the glittering figure of Neptune seems to urge on the brightly liveried oarsmen of a bissona taking part in the parade.

Although the crews of the ceremonial bissone are experienced gondoliers, hired for the occasion by the city which also supplies their brilliant costumes, things do not always go smoothly on the day of the regatta. Gondoliers are used to rowing alone—or at the most in twos—and there is room for differences of professional opinions, as here, when they come to working in teams of six or eight.

By the flower-covered prow of their boat, tense and thirsty competitors anxiously await a judge's decision on a close race. The winners receive a cash prize—formerly a purse of gold—to be divided between the crew.

A caorlina strewn with blossoms sweeps past a grandstand of costumed dignitaries, including Venetians dressed up as a doge and the Queen of Cyprus (centre). Among the prizes awarded is one for the best decorated boat.

Rowers' Hard-Won Fame

Most of the regatta contestants are professional gondoliers, but they still have to undergo rigorous training for the day. They compete in dozens of races during the summer, many of which are qualifying trials that produce finalists for the big event. Rivalry is intense: each crew is supported by ardent followers and the final winners become popular heroes, famous in towns up and down the Venetian lagoon.

Along a route lined with spectators and the painted poles that mark the mooring rights of palazzi, the regatta's Grand Parade sweeps onwards. The gondolas taking part in the regatta are not exactly the same as those that ferry tourists to and fro; instead they are special lightly built racing craft called gondolini. But the shape is the the same, the gracefully curving outline of the vessel that is called the "soul and symbol" of the city.

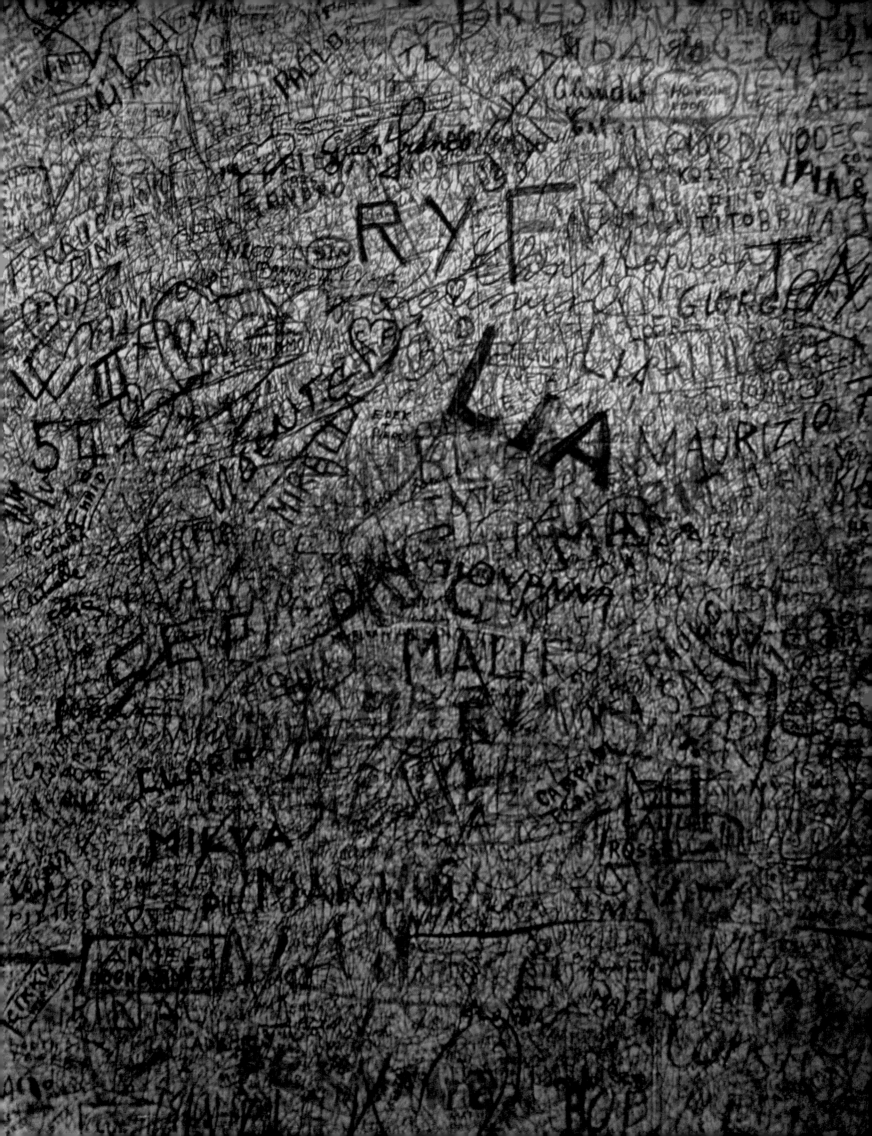

4

Signs of Change

The Venice of Goldoni is in the past. We must return to the present. That should be simple; but it is not—at least, not in Venice. The city exudes nostalgia, like a packet of old letters found in an attic. As every foreigner says, during his first three days there, Venice is a place in which to dream. It also has a built-in alarm clock to wake you up—the bill.

The hotel, then, has presented us with that sharp reveille, and, having paid it, we step out firmly into the 20th Century. As we do so, we are jostled by streams of tourists. Tourists, who observe a tight schedule, walk behind their guides at a peculiar trot. It is not quite as fast as that of the Italian *bersaglieri* when they are on show, but it is a trifle more swift than belated commuters hurrying to catch a train. In any case, it is wise to step out of their way, preferably on the non-aquatic side of the road. Already we are far from the footmen and the candelabra.

Venice does still try to recreate some semblance of its glorious past. Every two years, the city stages a great show of the arts, including that of the theatre. I went to the latter, and that was the end of another dream.

I did not go by gondola. La Fenice was closed, and its modern substitute was on an island in the lagoon. To the directors of the Festival (called the Bienniale) who are nothing if not slap up contemporary, La Fenice is an impossible place, with its picture-stage proscenium and its frivolous decor, not at all suited to modern seriousness. No gondola then, but a ferry in need of a coat of paint, which chugged its way out of the seductive delights of the old Venice to the bleak island, where the wind blew. It was so cold (although this was only September) that I felt I must be in Russia. I suspect I was *meant* to think of Russia. At this point I must explain the great change that has come over Italy and Venice in recent years. It started with the Italians' invention of Fascism of which they are now thoroughly ashamed. During Mussolini's day, corpulent civil servants were obliged to dress up as dashing soldiers in breeches. A friend of mine, the Contessa Gonfalonieri, finding herself the wife of a Fascist ambassador, would write on her official invitation cards, "Please leave your daggers on the hall table, because they frighten me." Naturally, the reaction to this somewhat farcical regime was deadly seriousness. And so it is today to Fascism's successor, Marxism, and with seeming inevitability, Italy has turned from far Right to far Left. Venice is now dominated by Marxists, some of whom, on the municipal council, are influential Communists.

So arriving at our island, we are not surprised to find that our "theatre" is far from a bourgeois affair of gilt and plush. It is a disused warehouse.

Layer upon layer of initials, dates, declarations of love and names in countless languages blanket a corridor wall in St. Mark's, testimony to the enduring attraction Venice holds for romantics of all nationalities—and to their compulsion to leave their mark on the city.

The show is staged by a director from Eastern Europe, at an expense (the taxpayer's expense) that would have made Goldoni's mouth water. On this occasion the audience sits not on plush chairs but on bare benches. There are no programmes, but that is because the famous director has disagreed with the ideology of the programme-notes and peremptorily scrapped the lot at the dress-rehearsal. As for the show, it is made up of snippets from the classic dramatists that are supposed to have modern social significance. And the lines are recited wholly in "ancient Greek".

This impresses me no end. As a small boy I was taught Greek for a few months, until my parents put a stop to it because it made my nose bleed. Listening to the actors cavorting and roaring up and down the warehouse floor, I remember that my schoolmaster cynically informed his little pupils that nobody had the least idea of how the Greeks pronounced "ancient Greek". This does not deter the actors from demonstrating that capitalist war is a Bad Thing. To prove this, a Second World War tank is brought on. I agree that this is a Bad Thing (I have always thought so) and creep out to the local bar where I watch, on television, an American detective story dubbed into Italian. Going back on the ferry, I feel colder than ever.

It was not always like this, and Venice is not always cold. In the summer months there is one part of Venice that enjoys a pleasant climate, sunny, but cooled by sea breezes; and here, on and off over this century, a film festival of varying extravagance has been held every couple of years. Its fate parallels that of Venice closely. The setting is a long, narrow island called the Lido. The Lido is a sort of breakwater between the sea and the lagoon on which Venice proper is built. A great deal of ecstatic prose has been written about the Lido by our fathers and even grandfathers, who regarded this strip of *terra firma* as the epitome of romance. For myself, I prefer the description contained in the vast Italian *Guide to Italy* (which runs to no fewer than 23 close-printed volumes). It suits today. The Lido, the guide tells us, is ideal for people suffering from gout and rheumatism, and especially those "suffering from exhaustion from excessive mental work". The picture of holidaymakers who do not want to walk, hob-nobbing with people who do not want to talk, has a certain bizarre attraction. And it is no place for hearty visitors who dash shouting into the sea. One must walk, the guide-book precisely informs us, a quarter of a mile before the water comes up to one's waist.

But what about the malady the guide-book describes as "suffering from excessive mental work"? We are all victims of this disease, whether it is caused by a long season spent trying to pick winners from a racecard or, as in my case, from hours sitting on a hard bench listening to "ancient Greek". The day following my experience in the warehouse theatre I went by steam-boat to the Lido. The island is by no means a place for solitary walks among olive groves of endless age, as one might imagine from the description in the guide-book. Today it is simply beach, corralled off into

To visitors, St. Mark's Square is an exciting first stop on a sightseeing round of Venetian glories. To Venetians who live near by, like these ladies perched on a bench fixed to one of the square's historic buildings, it is a community meeting place where local news is exchanged with friends.

sections and backed by the usual Maginot Line of hotels—a place, in a word, that one regrettably can find nowadays anywhere along the shores of the Mediterranean. And there were the usual tourists, in their thousands. I at least had the satisfaction of knowing that whereas if they pushed me into a canal I would get wet all over, here, if they pushed me into the Adriatic, I would get wet only to my ankles.

A German writer of genius (who was much given to overwork) set one of his greatest stories here. *Death in Venice* tells of a tired German writer who goes to the Lido to recover, at the beginning of this century. There were not so many hotels then, but there were a few, mostly filled with Germans, who were accustomed to bringing their children in the summer, no doubt because it was less easy for them to drown there than in the North Sea.

He stays in a hotel. Now Venice, as we have seen, had the reputation of being a wicked place. Corruption for Thomas Mann, who wrote the story, was in the very air; and in case we should miss the point, Mann stirs in a cholera epidemic. The visiting writer falls in love with a young boy—a frustrating experience that in no way helps cure his mental exhaustion. Watching the boy on the beach, he dies—whether from a heart attack, cholera, writer's block or the wrath of God, is not clear. Luchino Visconti made a visually beautiful film about it, and the cause of death is not made any clearer. But Thomas Mann's masterly story confirmed Europe's belief that, in the wicked city of Venice, the most dangerous place was the Lido, where one was not safe from temptation, even sitting quietly in a deckchair. I have no idea whether this was true at the turn of the century because I was not born then. But I do know that it is nonsense today.

During the First World War the Lido was, of course, deserted. But in the Twenties it sprang to life. Young as I was, I saw this re-birth, because my parents took me there. The Lido became the height of fashion, a sort of spaghetti version of the French Riviera, which was becoming uncomfortably crowded with war profiteers.

The Lido's revival was greatly helped by the Venetians' return to their first love, the drama. But now it was not drama played out in front of Goldoni's painted canvas, but the cinema, then at its glossiest. Each year, producers, directors, actors and actresses descended on the little island, with cohorts of photographers. Parties were incessant; champagne was guzzled, and one could not walk along the promenade without tripping over sweating, cross starlets, and being shouted at by even crosser cameramen. While we stayed only a day or two (because of the expense), I was always unhappy. What annoyed me most was that I could never get to see a film, this privilege being reserved for an elite with invitations, although some of them with the precious cards did not look, to my young eyes, as necessarily elite. What vexed me most was that, back home in one evening I could see two films, one newsreel and a cartoon for sixpence. And they were the same films.

Nevertheless, for the actresses and producers it was all a tremendous success. Cinemas were opened in England and called The Lido (pronounced by the Cockney as Lie-Doe), and the reputation of the festival spread wide. When the shadows of the Second World War began to draw in, the Lido fell once more on hard times. I was not particularly sorry.

The Second World War came and went, leaving the Lido forlorn and deserted. The whole civilized world was tired of austerity, death and ugliness. And, as had happened after the previous conflict, there was still money about. Those who had it dreamed of reviving the Twenties, that period of lavish expenditure and careless morals about which, nowadays, there is so much nostalgia. What better place could be found for this re-birth of gaiety than the Lido?

The film festival was revived. From all over the world (but principally from America) the still-rich came and re-opened the palaces. Expert public relations men from Hollywood were hired to recreate the parties, the receptions and the glittering guest-lists. The one hero of the war who was

In startling juxtaposition, clenched fists on a Communist poster show through the doorway beneath the family arms of Francesco Foscari, the wealthy 15th-Century Dogo who once resided in the palazzo. The building is occupied today by the economics institute of Venice university.

an undoubted aristocrat was invited to take part; Winston Churchill came and added his lustre to the hired footmen, the hired gondoliers, and the hired palaces on the Grand Canal. Lights blazed once again, the candelabra only a little dimmed by the omnipresent Klieg lights.

The Venetians willingly loaned out their beautiful city, dressed up the taller of their sons in footmen's uniforms, provided their gondoliers with brand-new waist sashes, and supplied the roisterers with more food and drink than was good for anybody. Then, with that Venetian scepticism that we noted when we went to that Goldoni first-night, they waited to see which way the cat would jump.

The cat, with considerable practical sagacity, jumped out of the whole charade. The Italian people had emerged from the war impoverished, bewildered and, over vast areas of the country, hungry. A withering blast of reality proceeded from the Press and the politicians. And when the carnival air spread from Venice to the capital, Rome, a film director from the provinces, shocked to his respectable provincial core by what his high-living fellow film-makers were doing to his country, produced a fable called *La Dolce Vita*. Although it had little to do with Rome, it was nevertheless so well made that it swept Federico Fellini to international fame, and put an end to the whole business. The film carnival was over, never to be revived either in Venice or in Rome. The Italians turned to the business of making motor cars, refrigerators, television sets and excellent imitations of English tweeds. They took due notice of Winston Churchill's warning that the Communists were the coming force in the post-war world, and accordingly gave that party an increasingly solid backing in every democratic and free election.

So the film festival, while it still holds forth on the Lido, is now quite a different matter, as I discovered when, on my last visit to Venice, curiosity prompted me to attend it.

There were, of course, no footmen. All the running dogs of capitalism were safely at home in their kennels, and wisely too, since anybody who displayed any sign of wealth stood the risk of being kidnapped and held to ransom. There were no jewels, no evening gowns, no elegant evening suits for the men (known, to the new Italians, by the derogatory word *frac*). As for the available food, I cannot judge. Something or other was laid out at intervals on long tables, but I never got near them in time to sample the offerings, being brushed aside in the stampedes. The films, mainly from behind the Iron Curtain, were as devoted to conveying messages as the vanished page-boys in Thomas Mann's Lido hotels. If I did not get the message, it was my own fault. Long evenings were devoted to discussing the films and their directors. As far as I could gather from the heated young men who monopolized these debates, the directors inevitably betrayed something or other and in the end were doubly suspected of wanting to make pictures of which the public approved.

Commerce by Canal

There are only two ways to get around in Venice: walk or float. Everything that is elsewhere delivered on wheels goes by boat in Venice. Each morning freight vans queue up on the city's causeway approach, waiting to transfer their loads to barges. Meat and vegetables, dresses for boutiques and medicine for chemists, wine, cigarettes and newspapers move along 28 miles of canals to the shops. Transport vessels emblazoned with signs advertising familiar trademarks chug past Italian Post Office parcel boats and brick-laden builders' barges.

For short trips along narrow pavements, Venetians use their feet. But the Grand Canal has only three bridges and were it not for cross-canal ferries a pedestrian bound for a place just a hundred yards away might have to make a detour as much as a mile long. Over 50 water-buses (*vaporetti* and the faster *motoscafi*) provide cheap public transport for longer journeys and 150 motorboat taxis ply for hire. There are only about a hundred privately-owned passenger motor launches in Venice.

Gondolas, of course, are everywhere—some 460 of them. But since they are costly to hire they usually carry tourists, not Venetians making their daily rounds.

A bargeman delivering bottled water takes a crate of empties while making his round of bars and cafés.

In the morning mist a woman going to market and two workmen avoid long, roundabout walks over bridges by taking a gondola ferry across the Grand Canal.

Fuel deliverers shovel coal into a basket and haul it up to canal-side houses.

A boatman in oilskins rows on waters darkened by shadows of rainclouds.

But I must admit that one problem of my boyhood had been solved. I had been angry then because I could not get in to see the films without an invitation. Such capitalistic, elitist, bourgeois customs had been abolished. The films (or some of them) were shown free in the evening in Venice's small squares. There, fishermen, gondoliers, vegetable vendors, and anybody on the way home to watch television could pause and imbibe the message. A very cautious poll that I took among these spectators revealed the complaint that, compared with the old days, all the female film-stars were remarkably ugly. *Sic transit Gloria Swanson.*

The day after I had watched the film, I went in the morning to Florian's, the café in St. Mark's Square. The sun was shining, although in the night it had rained; the bronze horses were still wet, as though fresh from a chariot-race in Byzantium. I stirred my coffee and wondered whether I had really come back to Venice to be educated in sociology, an education that I could get at much less cost in Belgrade, or Prague or Moscow. Had I really come all that way to see the *avant-garde* in the performing arts, which I could see much better in London or New York? If Venice was tired of itself, was I tired of Venice? I realized that I much preferred its former wicked self.

A Venetian friend, a neat man of some 40 years, came by and greeted me. In the Venetian fashion, he sat down at my table and accepted a coffee. I grumbled about my previous evening. He drank his coffee at a gulp and placed the cup firmly on its saucer. "We don't want Venice to become a museum city", he said. Then he got up, excused himself, and trotted off to catch a ferry to the island of Murano where he ran a glass factory.

When he had made his comment, I had nodded wisely. I always nod wisely when businessmen make pithy remarks, even though wise sayings of businessmen have cost me a lot of money when those remarks turned out not to be wise at all. For a few moments I watched the pigeons. Thousands of them were jostling towards some tourists, converging on them like football fans invading the pitch to get at the referee.

"But what", I said to myself, "is wrong with museums?"

Had I left my imagination behind me in my hotel bedroom? Here was everything to inspire it: unspoiled architecture, a timeless piazza. Suppose, instead of the manufacturer of glass bottles, the person who had sat and had his coffee with me had been somebody who knew Venice when it *was* the wicked city of masks and candelabra? It must be someone who knew the truth and was ready to tell me.

Not, therefore, a Venetian. They have never made it a practice to tell the truth to foreigners. Even among themselves it is a rare commodity, except under stress. When Marco Polo came back from China and told them about all that he had seen, they automatically called him a liar. Not until he had slit open his travelling suit and they saw jewels pour out on to the floor did they believe him.

Doorbells for 24 flats on a house where a single family used to live—and disused bell pulls rusting at the entrance to another once-grand dwelling—show the change that has overtaken many of Venice's old palaces.

The pigeons swerved *en masse*, and mobbed a very embarrassed schoolboy dressed in the uniform of an English private school. Then it occurred to me that there was one man who could have told me the truth about wicked Venice—an Englishman. Moreover, he had already told it. He was the poet Lord Byron. In a bewilderingly short space of time he had, as he said, woken up in England to find himself famous—and infamous—for he had published the first, controversial cantos of a poem, *Childe Harold*, and had been execrated soon after for being in love with his half-sister. This wicked man had fled to wicked Venice.

Besides being a poet, he had the gift of putting his thoughts down on paper, just as they came to him. The form he chose was letters. They were never long letters; in the early 19th Century it was the addressee who paid the postage, and Byron, ever a gentleman in the smaller things of life, confined himself to both sides of a large sheet of paper. I remembered having read them. This was the man I wanted to share my table—the chill wind of change in Venice being of a kind to force one back on fantasy.

I got up and went to a bookshop. I found the letters in an old edition in a shop frequented by scholars. I returned to the café. The sun was now higher in the sky. Tourists were wading ankle-deep in pigeons, but I took no notice of them. I read. And, in the mid morning sun, I dozed.

The figure that comes striding across the square towards me is familiar; perhaps it is the slight limp of the club foot. The mane of hair is rather restrained for an Englishman (although in his own times it alarmed his elders, who wondered what a world without wigs would be coming to). The open neck, with the wide wings of his shirt collar falling back on either side, is like that of his later countrymen among the pigeons. The tight trousers are, it is true, a little old-fashioned, although not unlike their American descendants, jeans. He is past his youth. He is growing, to tell the truth, a little corpulent. His manner of speaking matches his waist-line. It is plummy and rich, racy, even, for in his day the well-bred man imitated the accents of his jockeys and grooms; it expressed manliness. His grammar is, however, impeccable, not to say stately. It is the mark of his noble rank.

He sits at our table, with little ceremony. We delivered, yesterday evening, a letter of introduction from a certain young scribbler of verses named Percy Bysshe Shelley. Shelley is as big a scandal as Byron among the English, but Byron will have none of it. "The best and least selfish man I ever knew", he says, and since we do not react properly, he adds, raising his voice, "I never knew one who was not a *beast* in comparison." He rolls his famous eye at us and we are suitably subdued.

The waiter, without being asked, brings him a tall glass of some milky fluid. Byron runs his fingers through his hair and, changing his tone, says petulantly, with a great sigh: "I wish I was drunk. But I have nothing but this damned barley water."

Byron on barley water! That will be something to write home about. We watch him as, with grimaces, he drinks. We try hard to think of something that will impress the famous man, and come up (as is so often the case) with a question of the utmost banality. "My lord, how do you find Venice?"

We are not eaten alive. He is courteous. Perhaps he is happy to speak English, he who writes it so well. His Italian, we know, is fluent, but haphazard.

"The place pleases me. The *romance* of the situation—its extraordinary appearance . . ." He waves a delicate hand at the piazza, the church and the horses, ". . . together with all the associations we are accustomed to connect with Venice, have always had a charm for me, even before I arrived here." The famous glance again, this time very knowing. Aware, as is all Venice, of his romantic "associations", we look knowing too. "I have not been disappointed."

We take in his meaning. Here, if anybody, is the man who can tell us about wicked Venice. But not on barley water.

The great bronze Moors on the clock-tower strike the hour. The pigeons flutter into the air and drop back to earth and food. We call for a brandy, and find, as is the way with every poet on the wagon, no difficulty in getting Byron to join us.

What does he do to pass time? Besides, of course, writing immortal poetry?

He rambles, a bit boringly at first, like all expatriates. Then he knocks off the goblet of brandy.

"Then . . ."

"Then, my lord?"

"Then I have fallen in love with a pretty Venetian of two-and-twenty, with great black eyes. She is married—and so am I . . ."

We bury our nose in our glass. His rupture with his wife is the talk of London. We pass the test.

"Which is very much to the purpose", my lord sweeps on. "We have formed and sworn an *eternal* attachment . . ." A good long pull at the glass, and a slow smile, deep and Byronic (the fashionable adjective when we left London). "She does not plague me, which is a wonder, and I verily believe we are one of the happiest unlawful couples on this side of the Alps. She is very handsome, very Italian—or, rather, Venetian. Her spouse is a very good, kind man who occupies himself elsewhere."

He pauses. We decide to ask him straight out.

"We have heard, my lord, that in Venice morals are in such a happy state that . . ." We try a meaning but pause.

He turns on us the full force of the gaze that makes women fall at his feet.

"The general state of morals here is much the same as in the Doges' time. A woman is virtuous who limits herself to her husband and one lover.

Even ceremonial events in Venetian life involve a journey afloat: a newly married couple are photographed at the church before going by launch to the reception.

Those who have two . . ."

We refuse to be shocked.

". . . or three . . ."

We still refuse.

". . . or more, are a little *wild.*"

We nod. That is not the reaction that the wicked Lord Byron in wickeder Venice expects. He prepares, verbally, to knock us down.

"It is only those who form a low connection, such as the Princess of Wales with her courier, who are considered as overstepping the modesty of marriage."

We pretend to be knocked down. The Princess of Wales is Caroline, wife of the Prince Regent of England. Suitably embarrassed by this reflection on the British Royal Family, we signal to the waiter, who puts a bottle by the great man's elbow. It is not long before we persuade him to tell us what he is clearly wanting to narrate: the story of his latest female conquest. He is, after all, that archetype, an English expatriate. The lady's name (and as a gentleman he would never have mentioned it in London) is Marianna. He pours his brandy.

"A few days ago a gondolier brought me a billet without superscription intimating a wish to meet me. At ten o'clock I was at home and alone, Marianna having gone out with her husband. The door of my apartment opened and in walked a girl of about nineteen, who informed me that she was married to the brother of my *amorosa.*"

"Of Marianna, that is."

My lord nods.

"In a few minutes, to my very great astonishment, in walks Marianna herself. After making a most polite curtsy to her sister-in-law and me, without a single word she seizes her sister-in-law by the hair and bestows upon her some sixteen slaps which would have made your ear ache only to hear them. I need not describe the screaming that ensued."

The sister-in-law flees; Marianna faints.

". . . upon the sofa. After about an hour in comes—who? Why . . ." goes on the poet, lest we should interrupt "why—her lord and husband, and finds me with all the apparatus of confusion, dishevelled hair, hats, handkerchiefs, salts, smelling bottles, and the lady as pale as ashes. His question was, 'What is all this?' Oh, you need not be alarmed—jealousy is not the order of the day in Venice, and daggers are out of fashion; while duels on love matters are unknown—at least, with husbands."

He pauses, pours, drinks, and smiles—the first time that he has done so in our conversation. Like duelling, smiling is out of fashion with romantic poets.

"It was an awkward affair. He must have known I made love to Marianna, yet I believe he was not aware of the extent to which it had gone.

"I saw that he was quite calm. She went to bed, and next day—how they settled it, I know not, but settle it they did."

He sighs, a long, melancholic sigh. He pushes aside the brandy, and gazes at the barley water. He tosses back his hair in a magnificent way which, we suspect, he learned from Shelley, who was much given to the gesture.

"I did not dissipate much, on the whole, yet I find the sword wearing out the scabbard, though I have but just turned twenty-nine."

The bronze Moors on the clock-tower strike midday. We suspect that our dream in Venice cannot last until the twelfth stroke. Just so. My lord is getting up.

"So we'll go no more a roving", he says, in his beautiful voice. And he goes, upon the stroke of twelve.

Well, we have only been dreaming over a book of letters. We look around. We see the tourists and the pigeons, and return willingly to the book. What were his last words? "So we'll go no more a roving."

Here they are, just as he scribbled them down in Venice, on the night of February 28, 1817.

So, we'll go no more a-roving
So late into the night,
Though the heart be still as loving,
And the moon be still as bright.

For the sword outwears its sheath,
And the soul wears out the breast,
And the heart must pause to breathe,
And love itself have rest.

Though the night was made for loving,
And the day returns too soon,
Yet we'll go no more a-roving
By the light of the moon."

We close the book. We walk slowly by the arcades of the Doges' Palace. What we have read will last as long. Longer, perhaps.

5

A Delight to the Eye

Let us say that we have passed our three days in Venice. We must decide if we wish to stay longer. We walk out on our balcony in the morning to take a last look. If it is raining, we may well decide to leave—for Ravenna, or Florence, or Rome. But if it is not—if the sky is a pale, washed blue with white cotton-wool clouds, and if the water glitters as if alive with myriad fishes—we shall stay.

The mists swirl about the buildings and the buildings dissolve into the mists. And, as the sun gets higher, the colours come out, one by one—fresh, clean, like the colours emerging from a painting that is slowly being stripped of its yellowed old varnish.

You look, and look, and look; and looking, you stop thinking. "I do not seek; I find," said Picasso. In Venice *you* find, you paint with your *eyes* as they rove across the skies, the water, the palaces, the churches, the boats. It is just as well if you do not try to paint the scene with your hand, you have such titanic rivals among the Venetian masters of the past.

Since these giants—Bellini, Giorgione, Titian, Veronese, Tintoretto—distil the very essence of Venice, and since you have decided to stay, it is to them that I shall now turn your attention. Some days it is this special light shining down on Venice that has made Venice and painting inseparable. Venice, to a degree, *is* art. And we shall not know Venice to the full unless we know what this city did for its artists and what those artists did for art as we know it today.

Having passed our three days in Venice, we may well suppose that we—at least to the Venetians—"stink like a fish". On the other hand, those three days have taught us that the Venetians do not always mean what they say. We shall put their rude comment aside and stay. Having learned that Venice is a visual place, we shall, from now on, *look*, but not in wide-eyed innocence.

In the matter of painting, wide-eyed innocents are meat and drink, particularly to those who live by selling the work of artists. I have already mentioned the Bienniale. When the number of the year is even (1976, 1978, 1980, etc.), Venice holds an international exhibition of contemporary painting and sculpture, although the latter will not concern us. Critics, dealers and the public come from all over the world to see it, and the more advanced countries set up their own pavilions. Here, in the midst of a storm of controversy, back-biting and the sort of hysteria that goes with fashion shows, the most striking of current art is put on display. A prize is awarded and the fortunate winner is assured an excellent income

Visitors, like this man, can find fine works of art from every Venetian period at the Correr Civic Museum. Besides the wide variety of paintings, including portraits of doges and their retinues commissioned by the city from the best artists, the museum's collections include coins, documents, uniforms and weapons.

for several years, until he is forgotten in favour of another fortunate winner. The high prices that are paid for pictures by certain American artists are frequently due to the Bienniale, and not to the enterprise of New York gallery owners.

The point of my mentioning the Bienniale is that we must ignore it and all it represents. Those vast canvases consisting of splashes of colour that you see at exhibitions such as the Bienniale may well be the work of the Titian of our times. But they are not the work of the Titian of *his* times. That is altogether a different matter, which we are about to investigate.

When, in my adolescence, I first fell in love with Italian painting, I began—as we all do—by collecting anecdotes of the great. One in particular appealed to me. Titian was painting in his studio one day in the presence of the Holy Roman Emperor. He dropped his brush. The Emperor bent, picked it up and handed it back to him. The incident, it seemed to me, represented the epitome of artistic fame. Significantly, I now suspect that the story probably had another explanation. The Holy Roman Emperor was, I know, paying Titian a handsome retaining fee and his gesture might very well have been a princely hint to the old master to get on with the job, since he was known to dawdle over a canvas. Never mind: I was young at the time and impressed with the story. Thus inspired, I decided to go to a gallery, see a picture by Titian, select one area—the image, for example, of a dog—and say to myself: "I am now looking at the actual brush-strokes of the Master, the Dog as Titian painted him." I was very moved.

The Venetians brought home many sculptures as spoils of war to decorate St. Mark's, among them this porphyry group of four grim-faced chieftains—known as the Tetrarchs—now at the south-west corner of the cathedral. A 4th-Century work, probably of Syrian origin, it was looted from Byzantium and is thought to represent the Roman Emperor Diocletian (A.D. 284-305) and his three co-regents.

Not long ago I was looking at a Titian acquired by a museum as the result of a large outlay of public money. I would not now venture so rash a statement about any piece of it, unless I could go to the research and restoration rooms and examine the X-ray pictures of the canvas. That Dog of my youth may very well have been painted by a boy—an apprentice as young as I was, with no touch by the master save a few inspirational cuffs round the apprentice's ears.

To return to the Bienniale for a moment. When we look at modern art, we regard what we see on the wall as a work of self-expression; it is how the painter, and he alone, sees things around him. If it is nonetheless something that we, with our myopic eyes, can still recognize, all the better. If it is something we can never hope to see, because it is an interior world private to the artist, why then, so be it. We are trespassers who should not be prosecuted.

My point is that the more attuned we are to the art of our times, the more difficult it is to understand Giovanni Bellini, Giorgione, Titian, Tintoretto and Veronese. But we have already made a start. We have seen that the actors of the Commedia dell'Arte took pride in the fact that they were, first of all, artisans. They were skilled professionals, who used their gifts as custom and tradition prescribed. In the same way, painters of Venice, however talented they were, looked upon themselves, first of all, as craftsmen. They knew how to paint and they were anxious to paint what the public wanted. Moreover, they would—and did—paint on anything: walls, ceilings, even furniture.

Above all, The Worthy Ones wanted religious pictures, and they wanted them by the score. The favourite subject was the Madonna, because she was a woman, she was a mother, and she suffered. Some painters of Venice were perfectly happy to call themselves "Madonna-makers". They had no personal message. They did not look within themselves and find some highly original vision that they conveyed in paint. They had no messages, save those of the Church: they did not aim to shock, or astonish, or to be rebels against the Establishment.

Chagall's Paris studio—which I once had the good fortune to visit—struck me as a Holy of Holies where only he could work. Picasso's studio was guarded by security men and dogs. The studio of a Venetian painter, by contrast, had all the air of a busy workshop. Apprentices ran about at their master's bidding—grinding colours, setting up canvases, cleaning brushes, fetching food and drink. Meantime, they watched their employer at work. When they had used their eyes and heads enough to be able to paint on their own, their master would let them fill in a bit of the picture, provided they did it in his manner. As any portrait painter will tell you, once you have the pose, and painted the face and hands, there is a good deal of plain slogging to do: the clothes, the background, the chair, the carpet, and so on. These the brighter apprentices were allowed to do.

But they were not allowed to be too bright. A boy who was later to be famous as Tintoretto came into Titian's studio one day to learn how to paint. Titian quickly saw that he could already paint as well as himself and promptly threw him out.

Mostly, however, the apprentices were humble and obedient; if they had an inborn talent, they hid it until they had learned all the tricks of the trade. There was only one way of learning the techniques, and that was to work in the master's workshop. There were no art schools and no art teachers as such. If a painter knew of some way of making, for instance, a particularly attractive blue for the Madonna's dress, he kept the secret to himself—that is, for as long as he could. A sharp-eyed boy could discover it, perhaps, for himself; or, as often happened he could inveigle his way into the older man's affections and get what he wanted that way.

Above all, neither master nor pupils nor other painters sat around in the evenings talking about aesthetics. There were none. Aesthetics came on the scene only when the art of the Renaissance went into its decline. Painters worked all day, while the light lasted, and when it went they got drunk or went off to their mistresses or wives.

It is true that, elsewhere in Italy, when a painter became famous he would give himself airs. Michelangelo did so to such an extreme that his exasperated benefactor, Pope Julius II, was forced to hit him over the head with a stick to bring him back to earth. But egos did not easily inflate in Venice. The Venetian masters were not the sort to cut off an ear, like Van Gogh, or hide away in islands like Gauguin. Nor was there anybody (in Venice, at least) whose talent went unrecognized until long after his death. In a word, the Venetian painters were an unromantic lot. To find out anything about them we have to leaf through their invoices for work done or, as in the case of Titian, his extremely business-like letters complaining that he never got the money he thought was his due.

One can write novels, plays and films about Michelangelo or Leonardo da Vinci; there is plenty of material. There is virtually none about Bellini, Giorgione, Titian or Tintoretto. About Bellini we know little more than that he was a modest man. When his fellow artist, Antonello da Messina, came by with a new method—the technique of using oils—that had been discovered in Northern Europe, Bellini studied it like a young apprentice and changed his whole way of painting.

We thought we knew that Titian painted until he was more than 90 years old, but scholars have discovered that he exaggerated his age, so we do not know even that for certain. Giorgione is so obscure that it is only by a chance letter that we know he died young, possibly of the plague. As for his paintings, art critics have argued for centuries about which are his and which were done by assistants at his studio. There may be no more than 12 genuine paintings by Giorgione in existence, but we cannot be sure of even that number.

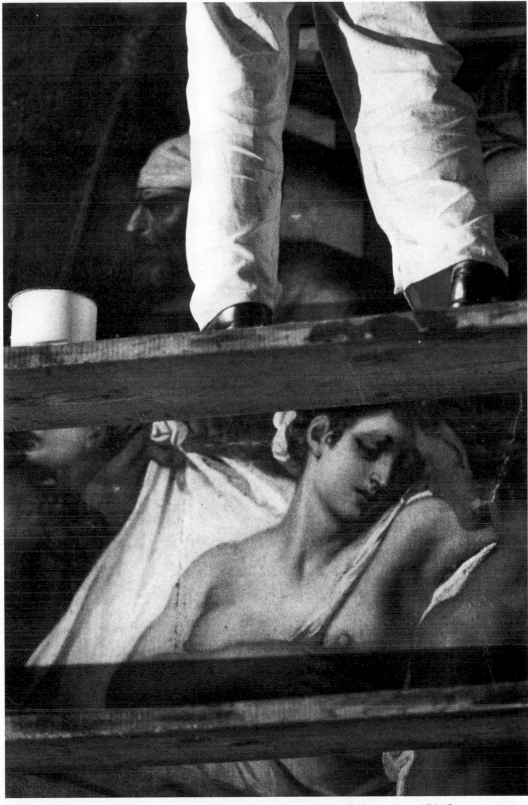

Perched high on a scaffolding, a restorer clad in workman's overalls attends to a huge 17th-Century painting.

The Fine Art of Rescue

Venice is an unparalleled storehouse of artistic treasures, yet the treasures—buildings, sculptures, paintings—are themselves in unparalleled danger. The most dramatic prophecies, like the total submersion of Venice within this century, are beginning to seem exaggerated, but the ceaseless threat from air pollution and dampness remains, calling for a constant investment of money and skill. The cataclysmic floods of November 1966 concentrated the horrified attention of the whole world on the city's plight, and brought contributions pouring in. With these it has been possible to expand the scale of conservation, until then only spasmodically undertaken. One aspect of the multifarious task—the care of paintings—is illustrated on these pages.

A restorer works on the extensive surface of a painting (right), brought in for restoration from the church of San Pantalon. The canvas is first mottled with tiny dabs of undercoat—an amalgam of chalk, plaster and colour—and covered over later with carefully matched paint.

One of a team of skilled painting restorers concentrates on finishing a new patch on a large 18th-Century work. He uses non-oil-based paint so that it will always be possible to distinguish on close inspection the restored parts from the original paint.

Crouching on a plank laid over the canvas, the restorer rules a large rectangle in chalk on a huge and badly damaged picture spread out on the floor for examination. The patch will be cleaned experimentally to determine whether the whole painting should be treated.

Furthermore, there is no drama even in the money side of these painters' affairs. They did not starve, like Modigliani; a successful Venetian painter was paid very well. Historians nowadays agree that—especially in our own financially uncertain times—it is meaningless to draw parallels, ducat by ducat and dollar by dollar or, indeed, in any modern currency. But we can compare social levels, and it is safe to say that a recognized artist in Venice got much the same financial reward as a respected doctor or admired surgeon gets over much of the world today.

Great paintings, undoubted masterpieces, are everywhere in Venice. In addition to the art galleries, there are the places where the artists used to gather—guilds, as we would call them, or perhaps trade union head-quarters. Confusingly, the Venetians called them *scuole*, "schools", although, as any visitor will quickly see, no school was ever decorated so lavishly. Besides such places, almost every church, however small, has something worth seeing. It is a paradox, but each year in Venice there are more paintings that should be seen—or rather, that *can* be seen. When I was young, many of them were so dirty and neglected that they were little more than dark brown oblongs, in dark rooms. Now, cleaned and lit (lit, that is, in the true Venetian spirit—you have to put a coin in a box for three minutes' worth of electricity in order to view them), the sheer volume of good painting in Venice is daunting.

Let us go back a moment to St. Mark's and look at a mosaic (page 103) that Bellini must have studied for hours. It is one of the undisputed master-pieces of Byzantine mosaic art and it tells us something about artistic conventions before Bellini began painting in oils. It shows Jesus entering Jerusalem. His entry was a popular triumph, to be followed soon by His crucifixion. The story is depicted with the greatest simplicity, yet nothing that is in the Bible is missed. Jesus rides upon an ass. Behind Him are His disciples. We can see three disciples in front, but behind them are nine haloes belonging to the others—in case anybody should start counting. Observe that everything about the scene is correct. If a television camera were observing the group, it could not see all of them. Some people are coming out of the city's gate. It looks rather too low but, if we resort to the device of our television camera again, we appreciate that a gateway behind a crowd would indeed look lower than the front rank of disciples. Some admirers carried palms; here is one doing exactly that. Another climbed a tree to get a better view; and there he is.

The most minute observation has been employed. The robes of the disciples flow backwards as they walk. Jesus sits acceptably in the saddle-cloth, His feet in the correct position. People had laid garments under the ass's hoofs and here they are, bunched where the hoofs fall. But all these details are outlined in a bold, clear strip of dark mosaic.

Everybody, including Bellini, must have recognized that a man riding on an ass is not seen with an outline around him, but the artistic convention

Details of two mosaics in St. Mark's Basilica demonstrate the vigorous linear style of Byzantine art. Such pictures—the one above shows Christ entering Jerusalem, the one below St. Mark—were intended to be other-worldly, and to inspire reverence in the beholder.

of the day demanded that he be outlined as a way of defining the body. The mosaic is such a splendid picture that the outline does not matter. In another mosaic—this one of St. Mark, in which the outline is not as well-rendered, it *does* matter. It is much too heavy. The knees and thighs of the Apostle look as though they have been confined in a metal band. All the same, it is an impressive portrait, and, if that was the way the Byzantines worked, who could do better?

The answer is the human brain could do better, especially when it was on the shoulders of a gifted artist; and those four apostles of Western painting, Cavallini, Cimabue, Duccio, and Giotto, had already begun to demonstrate this. But the brain could do better only slowly, step by cautious step, as it rid itself of old habits and preconceptions. To grasp the essence of Venetian painting and to see what Bellini, Giorgione and the other Venetian painters discovered, I invite you to follow the same cautious progress as they.

Let us return to the mosaic of Jesus entering Jerusalem. What did the man in the tree actually *see*? What would you have seen if you had been there? One of the great occasions of history, of course, but I am not addressing myself to religion. I want to discuss chemistry and electricity. In the real world, colours in the form of light were reflected by Jesus and the ass and, focused by the man's eyes, fell on an amazing collection of little tubes at the back of the eyes, the cones of vision, all infinitely smaller than the smallest pieces of a mosaic. The colour impinging on these individual tubes (like the electron beam striking the cells of a television screen) excites them. The tubes undergo a chemical change that produces electricity, which travels to the brain. Here other cells "name" the colour.

We now know that is *how* the man in the tree saw Jesus and the ass; he did not see them outlined. His visual tubes sent a tumble of messages back to the brain; these pieces of information, exactly like bits and pieces of a mosaic, consisted entirely of tiny patches of colour, which the brain put together as a series of bigger patches. By a process that is still a mystery, it called up all its resources of memory and reported that these patches added up to a man riding an ass. From the patches of colour, one beside the other, colours blending and fading into one another, the brain built up a picture *in the round*. Bellini knew that his eyes did not see what his hand had been trained to delineate; he knew it more than any other artist in Rome, or Florence, or Paris, or Amsterdam, precisely because he lived in colourful Venice.

I know of only one other place in the world where colours are so much the be-all and end-all. That is India. But to see them at their best you must get up very early in the morning, or even stay awake all night. By breakfast time they have been beaten flat by the tropical sun, surviving only in the flashes of the women's saris. As for seeing the Taj Mahal only by moonlight, the suggestion is not just a smart cliché; only then can its colours, most mysteriously, be seen.

Thus, Bellini and his pupils (some, as we shall see, themselves to become immortal) began to struggle with the notion that their expert hands were not telling the truth, as—unknown to them, and only partly known to us—their nerve-cells flicked and clicked messages from eye to brain.

Of course, much as they admired the mosaics in St. Mark's, they could also see other problems. Perspective was one of them. But finally it had become a simple matter; one had only to look at a canal through a large pane of glass. There was the scene, seemingly on the surface of the glass. With a brush one could put spots of paint where the chimney-pots were, the front doors were, and where the boats were tied up, tying them all together with receding lines. As far as the preliminaries were concerned, the thing was done, and the "study" could be copied on a panel or some other permanent surface.

Artists in Rome, Florence and all over Europe were absorbed in another conundrum. What did one really see when one looked at a human body? Leonardo da Vinci studied anatomy. Others studied the statues of antiquity. In Venice, there were no statues to be dug out of the mud; there was only this extraordinary spectrum of colours—in the air, in the clouds, above all the waters from which Venice had, like Aphrodite, arisen.

Before Bellini began his experiments with oils, Italian painters had but two media available to them: tempera and fresco. Almost everybody has a dab at painting nowadays, but few try these two methods because they are difficult to use. You can no more whip up a work in tempera while in an exalted psychological mood than you can dash off an inlaid mahogany

The 15th-Century Palazzo Foscari is on the Grand Canal. Yet the courtyard of the late Gothic building, with its cascading creepers and a classical statue among the oleanders, captures the atmosphere of a quiet glade.

table. Tempera colours come from the earth itself; powders of various hues that are held together by some gelatinous or sticky substance: with the early Italians the substance was usually the yolk of an egg. The result is art with a peculiar translucency. The brush strokes can be of the utmost delicacy, but they must be laid on by an artist who knows exactly what he is doing. It is difficult to correct mistakes (the corrections show), and a bold, slashing approach simply will not do.

Tempera paintings are much prized by connoisseurs, but for the general public they are an infrequently acquired taste. Many people do not care for the hard, dark outlines. (One of the many things the British disliked about Prince Albert, the consort of Queen Victoria, was that he collected early Italian tempera paintings. If they had known what a bargain he was buying for England they might have changed their minds.) Every great museum has rooms of tempera paintings, almost always of the calmer sort of religious subjects, and they are always the rooms most lacking a public.

The second principal method of early Italian painting was that of fresco. The Italian word (it means "fresh") describes the process. The wall is first covered with wet lime-plaster—a tedious job entrusted to the apprentices. The paint is applied directly to the wall. The colour source is the same as that of tempera—that is to say, earth pigments—but the colours must be put on before the plaster dries. The artist must work quickly and surely, with bold strokes; there is no opportunity to touch out mistakes. This annoyed Leonardo da Vinci so much that he invented an entirely new sort of paint to solve the problem. But he kept it secret; we do not know exactly what he used for his "Last Supper".

Then along came painting in oils. This method has the great advantage that colour can be laid on colour in semi-transparent layers called glazes, until an exact shade can be achieved; alterations can be made without showing, and whole areas can be scraped off and re-painted. The canvas or panel can even be set aside for years, if necessary, while the artist matures his design. Above all, oil records the master's actual brush-strokes, which are often as unmistakably his as a signature. This last advantage is the bane of all forgers. They can copy the design and the colours and even the composition of the colours, but they can never achieve the turn of wrist that was the master's own. They must resort to tentative dabs, and these show up under the X-ray like a disease.

We have learned that Antonello da Messina was the first Italian artist to use oils. On bringing the new technique to Venice, he revolutionized Venetian painting.

Messina—from which Antonello got his name—is a small town in Sicily, not noted for its artists. Near by is the beautiful town of Taormina. I lived in Taormina for the same length of time as Antonello stayed in Venice—that is to say, two years. Every Sunday morning I sat in the principal church within a few feet of one of his paintings. The subject was religious but I

This "Pietà" was the work of Antonello da Messina (c. 1430-1479), who made highly significant contributions to Venetian art. A Sicilian, Antonello is thought to have introduced the Flemish technique of painting in oil-based colours to Venice, where it was developed to glorious effect.

cannot say that it aided my devotions. It proved too cold. Antonello was clearly not greatly concerned with his holy figures (or with me). He was absorbed in technical problems, the chief one being how to render the human face and body as it really is—rounded. Like Bellini, he studied the gradations of shadows minutely. The effect on me was striking. As Sunday followed Sunday the figures seemed more and more to be made up of geometrical solids: cubes and cylinders, such as sit on shelves in modern art schools.

Antonello seemed to have had a monkish distaste for the fleshiness of the flesh. The Venetians, on the other hand, revelled in flesh. They wanted from the "Madonna-makers" pictures of the Madonna whose cheeks they could imagine stroking—if that were not too much of a sacrilege.

At the time of Antonello's arrival in Venice, Giovanni Bellini had carried the old style of painting in tempera about as far as it could go. He was admired by his fellow Venetians, but not as much as his brother, Gentile, who had an eye to the main chance. Gentile painted pictures of religious processions, that were not only elevating in moral tone but contained, in small portraits, everybody who was anybody in Venice. The figures are stiff and spiky. They derive, it is plain, from the mosaics in St. Mark's. But they were what the Venetians wanted and they were the sort of pictures that today would be snapped up by gallery-owners, whatever their artistic merit. Gentile left little mark on the history of art. His brother went his own way, experimenting with the new and exciting medium of oils.

Oil paints enabled Bellini to capture colour and all its many nuances, and to render form without outline. Letting his eye guide him, he created with his oils a whole new way of painting. He drew upon the soft light and varied hues around him to paint figures that appeared more real, more three-dimensional, than any that had been done before. Those Venetian artists who came after him advanced his technique, and it is their work we shall be looking at next and comparing to his.

Reflected Glory

Reflected in a canal's smooth surface, a hotel with gondolas moored in front assumes a graceful curve as its bright awnings smudge to an artist's softer red.

When Ernst Haas arrived in Venice to "dream around", as he says of taking pictures for this book, he was captivated as generations of artists before him had been by the colours and light reflected in the water of the canals. He perceived the water as a second lens with which to view the city. Peering down into the mirroring canals, he watched as Venice's shapes softened and dissolved in ripples. Only the gondola, the city's trademark since the Middle Ages, seemed to withstand complete liquefaction and retain its curving sweep in the water. Even the harsh metal structures of industry on the outskirts melted into elegant streamers. Suitably inspired, Haas began to photograph the reflections of Venice. In the resulting portfolio, the wavering images shift gradually from the recognizable (above) to the purely abstract.

White trim on a building translates to wiggly lines.

A mirrored row of gondolas shimmers.

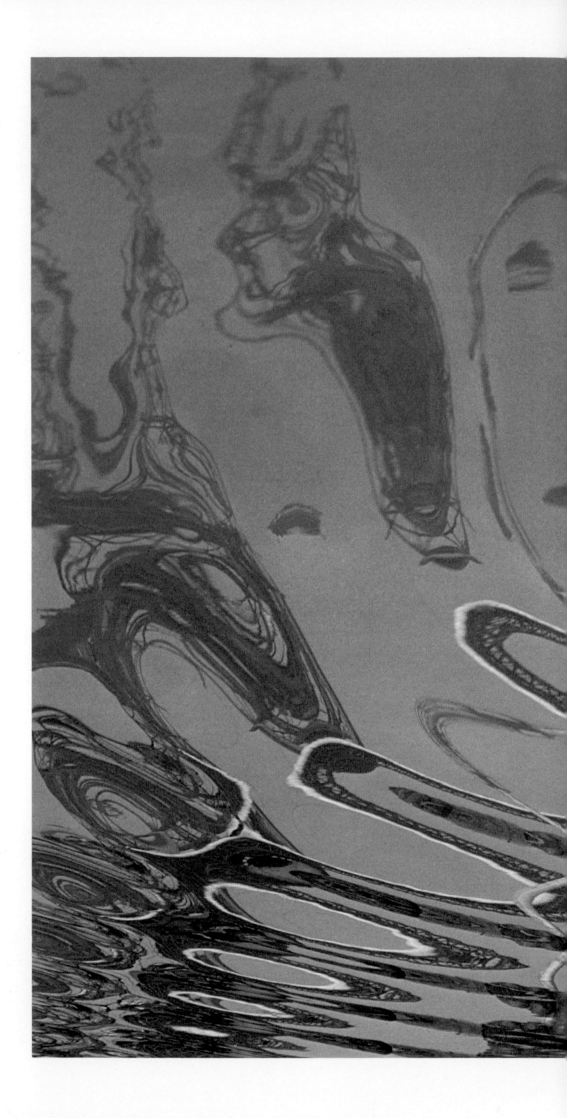

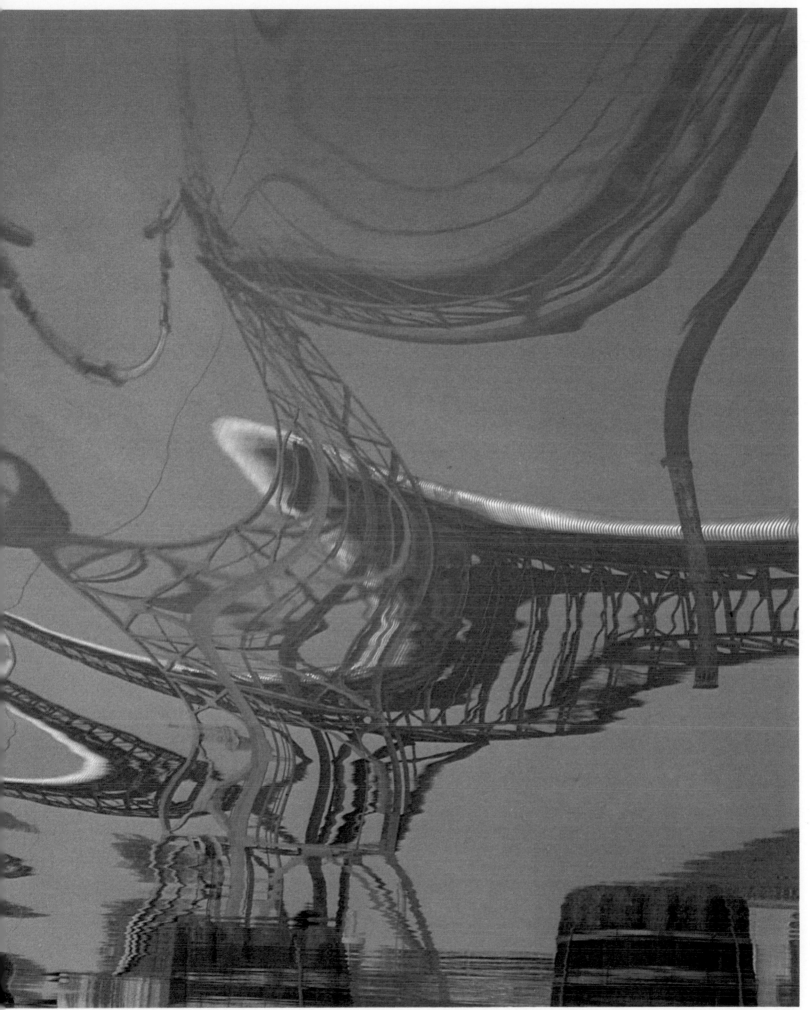

Steel cranes at Marghera bend into new shapes.

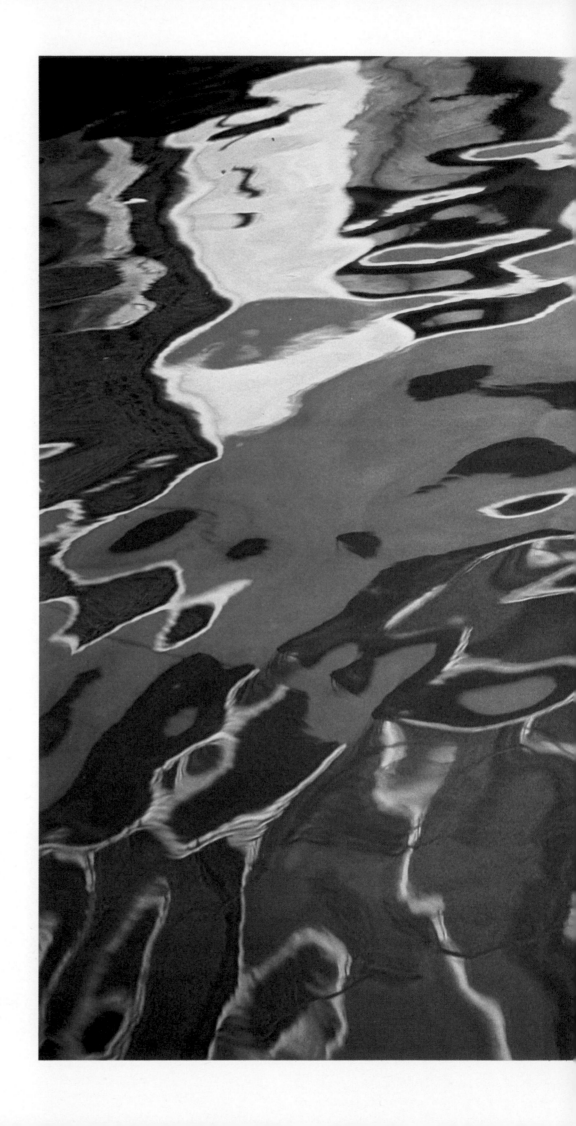

A mix of colours creates an abstract painting.

6

An Artistic Legacy

We are now going to make an expedition to see a picture. In most, perhaps all, of the famous cities of the world, this is a matter of individual choice. In Venice, it is a necessity. Of the five senses we possess, in Venice only one can be delighted to the full, and that, of course, is sight. The others do not fare so well.

The least said about smell the better. The narrow canals of Venice were designed in the belief that the Adriatic would sweep them clean. But the Adriatic is merely a part of the Mediterranean and, as we learned at school, the Mediterranean is nearly tideless. A good brisk wind can raise the water so that it floods, as we know, St. Mark's Square. But when there is no wind, there is a miasma. Of course, one does get used to it. One can also get used to the smell of a gas-works, or a tannery.

Hearing, as elsewhere in Italy, should not be too acute. Venice was once (so I am told) a quiet place. True it has no automobiles (they must be parked at the western edge of the city, but it has every other form of the internal combustion engine, as well as jets taking off and landing from the airport on the Lido. Little boys, playing in the squares, do not go "vroom vroom"; instead, they make a most realistic imitation of an outboard motor, the sound that is most characteristic of Venice in general.

The sense of taste, according to guide-books and travel articles, is one to indulge in foreign travel. The Victorians praised Venetian cooking, but then at home they lived on boiled beef and carrots. Years ago the Venetians were well-known for their fresh fish. Since really fresh fish now costs what our ancestors once paid for caviar, not much good fish should be expected in Venetian restaurants. In any case, nowadays the restaurants depend on groups of tourists who are grateful to sit down and take their weight off their feet, and are therefore disinclined to object to what is put in front of them. Venetian head waiters and proprietors are sympathetic to the gourmet's special order—or at least they pretend to be. They will listen respectfully. But you will get the same food from the same pots as the tourist group, which you can discover by going into the kitchen.

As for touch, today Venice is far more respectable than it even was in Lord Byron's day, when it earned its reputation for permissiveness, and more I need not say.

So we are left with our sense of sight, and there the city is triumphant. The eye dances with delight, like a child let out of school. Could I have ordered my life according to my wishes, I would have saved Venice until I had seen everything else; for, after Venice, everything else looks just a

Among pyramids of flowers a Venetian wedding is conducted in the Gothic church of Santa Maria dei Frari, built for the Franciscan friars between 1340 and 1469. Above the small figures of the participants towers Titian's "Assumption", a masterpiece of turbulent dynamism finished in 1518.

little drab. When I am very old and my sight begins to fail (which God forbid), I shall go back to Venice. I shall take the walk that we shall take now, and go first to see a picture by Bellini.

We walk by the Grand Canal, past the Doges' Palace, past the Bridge of Sighs, and past a building that once was a palazzo, where Alfred de Musset, Georges Sand, Charles Dickens, John Ruskin and Marcel Proust stayed. We do not give them a single thought. They were *writers*—aliens in this City of the Eye, nosing around for copy, no doubt.

We turn left from the lagoon and come, in a few steps, to what must be one of the most appealing squares in the world. Here is an arcade of exquisite proportions. There are the blazing colours of vendors' stalls, and filling one side, the façade of a church, San Zaccaria, set off by two great trees. We go inside but with no deep religious feelings. It was once a convent and, in the early 16th Century, the nuns had as good a time as Byron's Marianna. Their gaiety was not unusual for the period; in another convent of the time, the priest in charge of their immortal souls arranged naked bathing parties. In San Zaccaria, the nuns openly entertained their lovers, and, when the police tried to close the place, greeted them with a shower of stones.

So much for history; now for our eyes. There, in a side chapel on the left, hangs a picture of the Madonna with St. Peter, St. Catherine, St. Lucy and St. Jerome. It is a masterpiece of Giovanni Bellini, when he had learned to paint as his mind saw.

I shall not describe it. Even if I had the flow of words of any of those writers who stayed in the Palazzo Dandolo, I would not attempt to do so. Besides, it is reproduced here, on page 123, and I invite you to be thoroughly Venetian and to turn away from prose to *look* for a moment.

If I were tempted to chatter on about its composition, or any of its other delights, I would not. Besides, Bellini himself would put a finger to my lips to silence me, for in the middle of the picture there is an angel playing music on a viol—music not to be disturbed.

Only when we are once more in the square outside, with its noise and bustle, will I permit myself to say anything, and that in the same mood of release as when one applauds at the end of a symphony.

Bellini had found the thing he sought. In this painting there are no harsh outlines. We see as the cells of our minds see the world around us, with infinite gradations of colour—and in the round. As for myself, I shall turn and go back, as I always do, to look at the head of the saint who is reading a book. I approach closer and closer until I can see (yet I cannot *exactly* see) the strokes by which the master has passed from the light of day on the saint's face to the shadows under his cowl.

With Venice, you can change moods without compunction, day by day, almost hour by hour. There is no need to be consistent in Venice, and I do not mean to be. Thus, although I would not speculate in words about

Outside Quadri's, the famous café in St. Mark's Square where generations of visitors have sat, a violinist serenades the customers. Behind his attentively bent head rises the façade of St. Mark's, softly blurred in the late afternoon light.

Bellini, I shall now do so about his pupil, Giorgione, because that is clearly what the pupil wanted.

His real name was Giorgio da Castelfranco Veneto, which means that he was born (in 1478 or thereabouts) on the mainland—the Veneto. The Venetians took him to their hearts and gave him the nickname "Giorgione", meaning "Big George". This was a tribute to his extraordinary gifts as a painter but, given the humour of the Venetians, it may also have been a sly dig at the fact that he was extraordinarily fond of women and very successful with them.

If he knew about women, he also knew a good deal about putting himself over to the public; he had a knack for getting himself talked about. If I may briefly come forward to modern times, a gallery-owner I knew once advised me not to miss the opening of an exhibition by a talented and handsome young Spanish artist he had discovered. I went. It was plain, after a few minutes' inspection of his canvases, that he was indeed talented. Whether he was handsome or not was more difficult to decide, because he turned up at the show dressed in a deep-sea diver's suit. Why? Who was he? The gallery owner said his name was Salvador Dali. As for why he was dressed in a diving suit, he left that to us. The Freudians among us said, confidently, that it was to show that he was exploring the depths of his subconscious. The art critics said he wanted to hit the headlines. We were both right. Dali has been talked about ever since.

The polished marble floor of the west gallery in St. Mark's reflects two of the four bronze horses on the balcony, brought from Byzantium in the 13th Century.

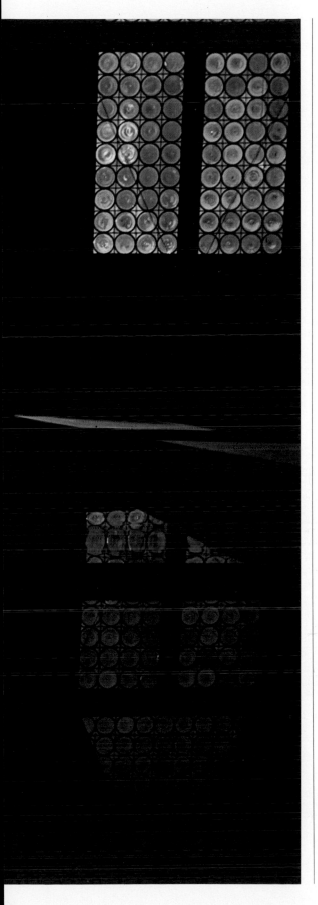

Giorgione adopted a more subtle method. He chose mystifying subjects. He painted them with the new technique of his master, Bellini, and improved upon it. His colours were even more blended into the shadows, and the shadows even darker than we have seen in Bellini's "Madonna and Child with Four Saints". All that he would say in explanation was that every single thing he painted came from a minute study of Nature itself. The result was landscapes, with figures, that had never before been seen in Nature. I do not mean that they were bizarre.

Everything could be identified—a tree, a rock, a bosom, a head. But hanging over each scene was a brooding air of mystery, made all the deeper because Giorgione did not identify the legend he was painting.

His most famous example of mystification is found today in the Accademia of Venice, the great art gallery built after the zenith of Venetian painting had passed, but which contains a fine survey of what had been done. The painting is called "The Tempest", although it was not given any name by Giorgione. A woman sits on a hillock. Behind her is a distant view of an Italian town with a bridge and towers. Over this hang the clouds of a storm, the colours caught as no man had ever caught them before—and few genuine artists would claim to have done it as well since.

Like a madonna the woman holds a child, but she is only partly dressed, her flesh mysteriously lit by the approaching storm. So she cannot be a religious figure. Some broken columns opposite her suggest that a classical story is being told, and she looks out of the canvas directly at us, as though challenging us to say what she represents. Down in the left-hand corner is the figure of a young soldier, leaning on his lance. If Giorgione ever dropped a hint as to the story he was telling it is certain that it was quite forgotten a mere 20 years after his death.

The painting has been argued about, through the years, almost as much as Leonardo da Vinci's "Mona Lisa". "The Tempest", according to many, is even better done. All the hardness of line that survived in Leonardo as a heritage of the past has gone. Colours flow into colours so that the picture seems alive, like water in a rippling pool. The coming storm—there is a flash of lightning—permeates everything, and to some observers it dominates the mood of the soldier and the woman.

What did Giorgione intend? Until recently wonderfully romantic suggestions have been offered. Nowadays we ask, instead, "Did Giorgione *himself* know what he meant?" This is due to a curious discovery. The picture was X-rayed and it was revealed that, under the soldier, Giorgione had originally painted a completely nude figure of a voluptuously curved woman. Then he had brushed her out and put in the soldier instead.

The woman is bathing her feet, and so far no romantic explanation of his mundane act has been offered.

Had Giorgione not created a mystery around himself, I think he would still have been eclipsed in our memories by Titian, another pupil of

Titian's sombre "Martyrdom of St. Lawrence".

Four Venetian Masters

The paintings reproduced here and overleaf are by four giants of Venetian painting: Giovanni Bellini (*c.* 1430-1516), Giorgione (*c.* 1478-1510), Titian (*c.* 1488-1576) and Veronese (*c.* 1528-1588). Working in oils, Bellini began to use colour in a more deliberate and effective manner than previous Venetian painters. Giorgione and Titian both followed Bellini's lead and became the chief creators of High Renaissance painting in Venice. Giorgione died young, a mysterious figure whose paintings combined limpid colouring with enigmatic atmosphere. Titian's exuberant creativity developed through several distinguishable styles during his long and prolific life. In the work of their less profound successor, Veronese, the Venetian love of colour and splendour reached opulent expression.

Giorgione's "The Tempest".

Giovanni Bellini's "Madonna and Child with Four Saints".

"The Triumph of Venice", ceiling painting by Veronese.

Bellini's. Even in his youth Titian was destined to be a giant among artists, and for all time. Giorgione could scarcely have failed to notice him because the young Titian set himself humbly to copy the famous man. He did so well that some of his early works were mistaken for Giorgione's.

I have said that a Venetian painter was a practical man ready to paint anything. In this instance, teacher and pupil were working on separate façades of the Fondaco dei Tedeschi, a warehouse for German merchants. Nothing remains of the work of either on the Fondaco, and the building is now used as the city's post-office. There are, nowadays, always long queues at the post-windows and interminable arguments. It helps one's patience to recall that this humdrum place was the cause of a celebrated quarrel.

Giorgione's work was, as usual, mysterious. The biographer, the 16th-Century Italian painter Vasari, who beheld the fresco when it was still fresh, threw up his hands in despair. He saw a woman and a man, another man with a lion's head, a dead giant and a woman raising a sword and speaking German. Vasari says frankly, "I cannot discover what they mean, whether they represent some ancient or modern story, and no one has been able to tell me."

Meantime, young Titian was working on the other façade, and it was Giorgione who had got him the job. We have seen that Big George was an open and amiable man, but that is a characteristic which, in any genius, must not be pushed too far. Some German merchants, obtusely unaware that Titian was also at work on the building, heaped compliments on Big George for his pupil's work, thinking it was the master's own. Giorgione sulked. He refused to appear in public until Titian had finished both frescos, a clear way of showing that they were not his. But he did not dismiss Titian, which in those days was quite a common thing to do to a rival. He made no attempt to stop the young man. I fancy that, short of stabbing him and throwing him into the Grand Canal (also a custom in Venice in these pre-Byronic times), nothing would have.

Titian's fame grew rapidly. He was summoned to Rome. Venice was always jealous of the power of the Popes, who were monarchs in every sense of the word. Rome was also jealous of the swelling reputation of the Venetian painters, with their new-fangled way of painting only with colours to mark the design. And what colours! Rome is not a colourful city. It is tawny, like a lion. Such colours as are to be found there are those of polished marble, a cold business beside the dazzle and warmth of Venice.

In Rome, in the Vatican palace, Titian met the greatest artist alive, Michelangelo. In spite of his other gifts, Michelangelo had only a restrained interest in colour. He praised the younger man but then remarked, "It is a pity you Venetians cannot draw."

But Titian could draw. He drew with a difference: with his brush—with a riot of colours that were without parallel in the history of art. Princes, dukes and even an emperor vied to buy his paintings. Not the least of the reasons for Titian's success was that he turned his attention to rendering the colours, the shapes and the softness of a woman's naked body. His women sit, stand, loll and sprawl in all the great museums of the world.

There are so many Titians to see in Venice that I shall select only one, in order that our art tour shall not degenerate into a mere survey. In the Church of the Jesuits there is a picture by him of the Martyrdom of St. Lawrence (page 122). It shows all of Titian's powers, but it is remarkable for one thing. Titian, having painted light (for colour is light) as no one before him, turned to painting darkness. There is a flicker of torches, a beam from heaven, and a glowing fire. All the rest is in thick, dark colour, like the shadows in the folds of a velvet robe. With this achievement he began a whole new school of painting.

The last great period of Venetian creativeness has no parallel until we come to the American film director Cecil B. de Mille. De Mille loved crowds and he had the money to hire them. The Worthy Ones loved crowds just as much, and they had the money to hire artists to paint them. De Mille discovered History and, since it was far from satisfactory as a scenario, had it re-written. History had already been discovered by the Renaissance, especially the glories of ancient Greece and Rome. Here, too, the records proved to be unsatisfactory, since the Greeks and Romans were, by Venetian lights, decidedly niggardly with the money they spent on their clothes. This was put right very rapidly by artists such as Veronese and Tintoretto, who set about painting the heroes and divinities of the classics in the sort of costumes that were proper for Venetian ladies and gentlemen.

Veronese was born in 1528 and died 60 years later. The enormous amount of work he turned out in those years must be judged anew by each generation. In his lifetime he was compared to the greatest painters who had ever lived, and he certainly had no doubts about himself. When the English replaced the Venetians as the people who had enough money to afford art, they bought Veronese avidly. The result was that eventually his paintings could be found all over the world; it is not too much to say that an art gallery cannot be considered worthy of the name unless it has at least one of his pictures.

I have noted much the same about Titian. But there is a difference. Titian can be understood in a foreign gallery. Veronese, and his rival Tintoretto (1518-1594), cannot. They must be seen in Venice. I would go further: one of the principal reasons for going to Venice is to see their work and make up your own mind about them. As in the case of Bellini and Giorgione you need the colours, the light, the waters and the skies of Venice to prepare you for them. They cannot be savoured by going into a gallery from the wind and rain after munching a lunch-time sandwich.

An elderly Venetian who had known his city when there was still money

The Rise and Fall of Venice

452	Invasion of Italy by northern Barbarians forces mainland Italians to take refuge on islands of Venetian lagoon. Founding of Venice
466	Election at Grado of first Tribune to govern affairs of each island. Refugees from mainland adapt themselves from agriculture to fishing
539	Justinian, the emperor in Constantinople, sends Belisarius to conquer Italy; he enlists support of Venetians to defeat Ravenna, so beginning relationship between Venice and Constantinople
568	Lombards invade Italy and new refugees join first settlers on island of Torcello
584	Venetians refuse to submit to emperor in Constantinople but promise him co-operation
697	Patriarch of island of Grado calls assembly of lagoon people and first Doge is elected to govern all islands
811	To escape warring Franks, seat of government is moved from Torcello to island of Rivo Alto (today's Rialto) in the middle of lagoon
1063-1073	Basilica of St. Mark built in its present form
1172	Election of Doge and Councillors placed in hands of Great Council, elected by 12 Tribunes
1204	Venetians undertake to transport members of 4th Crusade to Holy Land but when these are unable to pay, compel them to assist in capture and sack of Constantinople. Among the loot brought back, four gilded bronze horses, still in position on balcony of St. Mark's
1271-1295	Marco Polo, a Venetian, travels overland to China and back
1297	Great Council eliminated and substituted by new Assembly drawn from noble families whose names were inscribed in the "Golden Book"
1335	Power of State concentrated in ten members elected by the noble families
1342	Richest enamels and precious stones from Constantinople assembled to form altar screen for St. Mark's known as Pala d'Oro
1379-1381	Genoa's attempts to deprive Venice of her foreign monopolies and territories ends with defeat of Genoa in War of Chioggia
1402-1408	Venice expands empire on Italian mainland almost to Trieste in the north and Verona in the west to protect trade routes

1430 Contract signed by Marino Contarini with architect Marco d'Amadio for building of the Ca' d'Oro, the once gilded palace on the Grand Canal considered best example of Venetian Gothic

440-1500 Early Venetian Renaissance, centred mainly around paintings of Giovanni Bellini (c. 1430-1516)

1453 Fall of Constantinople to Turks, making access to eastern trade routes more difficult for Venice

1498 Discovery by Portuguese navigator, Vasco da Gama, of the sea-route to India. Venice loses its dominant position in trade with the East

500-1540 Height of Venetian Renaissance marked by masterworks of Giorgione (c. 1478-1510) and Titian (c. 1488-1576)

1508 League of Cambrai instituted by European powers to prevent further expansion of Venice

537-1554 Sansovino Library erected opposite Doges' Palace— one of Venice's most admired Renaissance buildings

550-1600 Use of colour and light in Venetian painting developed to full by Veronese (c. 1528-1588) and Tintoretto (c. 1518-1594)

1571 Turks defeated at the battle of Lepanto by an alliance of Venice, Spain, Genoa and the Papacy

574-1577 Fires damage the interior of the Doges' Palace
1576 Typhus plague takes heavy toll of Venetians

1592 Consecration of the Church of Il Redentore, built by Andrea Palladio to commemorate end of the plague

630-1686 Santa Maria della Salute constructed, after plague of 1629

707-1793 Carlo Goldoni writes comedies portraying decadence and decline of Venetian mercantile society

720-1790 Tiepolo (1696-1770), Canaletto (1697-1768) and Guardi (1712-1793) bring Venetian art to its final flowering

1797 Invasion of Venice by Napoleon. Abdication of last Doge and death of Venetian Republic Venice ceded to Austria

841-1846 Construction of railway link between Venice and mainland

1866 Austrian domination ends when Venice becomes part of the new kingdom of Italy under Victor Emmanuel

1966 Disastrous floods focus world attention on fact that Venice is slowly sinking into the sea

971-1972 Loan of 250 thousand million lire raised under auspices of UNESCO for purposes of rescuing city from damage by floods and pollution

to throw about has told me that the only way really to enjoy Veronese is to look at his work when you are full of wine, food, and in fancy costume for a masked ball. I am sure he caught the essence of the matter.

Veronese is everywhere in Venice—in its churches, its palaces and its galleries. My note-books show that I have seen no fewer than 30 specimens of his art. At least, I have stood in front of them. Nobody can actually *see* that amount of picture-space, much of it swarming with figures. And Tintoretto turned out even more paintings—nearly twice as many.

How good was Veronese? I have gone round Venice with an artist who was exhibiting, with renown, at the Bienniale. He belonged to what he himself called the dribble-drabble school, as far from Veronese in style as can be imagined. He said that Veronese was not only good, he was too damned good.

I accept that judgment. Veronese came at the end of a long line of Venetian masters who had spent their lives in experimenting. He had learned everything they had to teach him. Composition came to him as easily as it did to Mozart, or Shakespeare who "never blotted a line". Colour was in his veins and at his bidding poured out of his brush. He could marshal hundreds of figures on his canvases with the deftness of— well, there is no way of avoiding the comparison—de Mille.

For the last product of the Venetian genius in painting that we shall look at together, let us return to that ceiling in the Palace of the Doges and look at the "Triumph of Venice" (page 124). When we saw it then, it bewildered us. Now we know more. Let us check what we know; the wealth of Venice, the pride of its great families, the Venetian belief that there is nowhere like Venice, the love of pomp, the love of crowds, of fine clothes and parties. So, we look up once more at the ceiling.

Instantly we see why the contemporary artist had called Veronese too damned good. The whole thing could not be done better. The perspective is insolently perfect: the colours sing in unison, the whole riotous composition sits perfectly in the most difficult of all shapes for an artist: an oval frame. Any painter might well feel that Veronese had left him nothing more to do.

"Venice" sits on her throne (the picture is also known as the "Apotheosis"), plump, arrogant and unashamedly showing off her incipient double chin to us mortals down below. She is swathed in clothes, but if you want bare flesh, there is a nude attendant. Two spiralling pillars show Veronese could do anything he wanted with architecture (except invent it; he stole the design from St. Peter's in Rome). Between them, on a terrace, is that Venetian delight, a party with great ladies and important men—The Worthy Ones at play. Then, below, come the people, admiring two prancing horses, ridden by men in gorgeously inlaid armour. They represent the martial prowess of Venice, as similar actors did again and again in Venice's endless processions. Lastly, there is a dog. It is a very fierce dog, ready to bite someone except that a servant is holding it back.

The dog is a miracle. You look at it with relief, after all that is going on above. But your eye is carried back—how I will not venture to explain—to Venice triumphant. This is exactly what Veronese intended, and what The Worthy Ones paid for.

Without knowing it, perhaps, they got much more. They made Venice immortal, while they themselves soon disappeared into dust. Who remembers the names of the Doges, except specialist historians working on grants? Venice was proud of her fighting valour against the Turks; she struck lusty blows whenever she was not striking bargains with them. But who remembers the names of her warriors? There is the mercenary Colleoni, but he survives because of the statue of his horse. And, without a doubt, the Venetian general most famous in all the literate world is a black who murdered his wife and never existed—Othello the Moor.

In its last great days, Venice gave its painters a prestige that enabled them to face up to the terrors of the Inquisition, that powerful religious body that made even Galileo deny (whatever he may have muttered to himself) his belief that the earth went round the sun. Can we, in the West, claim as much when our geniuses got into difficulty with authority? Oscar Wilde? James Joyce? Ezra Pound? Or, to go East, Solzhenitsyn, and those unnamed Soviet painters who cannot show their pictures in Moscow without the fire-brigade being called out?

Consider what happened when Veronese ran foul of the ecclesiastical authorities. He had painted a vast canvas portraying the Last Supper when, according to the New Testament, Jesus instituted the ceremony of breaking bread and drinking wine in memory of His death. Veronese had turned the event into the sort of thing that pleased both him and his pay-masters: a rip-roaring Venetian feast. The Inquisitors were shocked and summoned him before them. It must be remembered that they had the power, supported by the Pope, of imprisoning him for life as a heretic; they even had the right to extract a confession from him by torture. But there was this important difference, and one vital to any person who would understand what Venice has meant in the history of our civilization. Before the Inquisitors brought Veronese to trial, they had already agreed that The Worthy Ones could be present at the trial and withhold any sentence the ecclesiastics should impose.

Venice, the Session of the Inquisition Tribunal of Saturday, the 18th of July, 1573. Veronese had painted in figures, to wit, a soldier and others, that formed no part of the orthodox version of the Last Supper.

Question: Do you know the reason why you have been summoned?

Answer (from Veronese): No, sir.

Question: Can you imagine it?

Answer: I can well imagine.

Question: Say what you think the reason is.

(Veronese rambles, as who would not? Imagine the cowled figures, the armed guard, the crucifix.)

Question: Have you painted other Suppers beside this one?

Answer: I painted one in Verona. I painted one in the refectory of the reverend fathers of San Giorgio, here in Venice. I have painted one in the refectory of the Servi of Venice, another in the refectory of San Sebastiano in Venice . . . .

(Let us pause to remember where those pictures of the accused are today—in the galleries of Turin, and two in that shrine of our culture, the Louvre in Paris. They question him now about his "Last Supper", made for the church of San Giovanni and San Paolo.)

Question: What is the significance of the man whose nose is bleeding?

Answer: I intended to represent a servant whose nose is bleeding because of some accident.

Question: What is the significance of those armed men dressed as Germans, each with a halberd in his hand?

Answer: This requires I say twenty words.

Question: Say them.

Answer: We painters take the same licence as poets and jesters take. I received the commission to decorate the picture as I saw fit. It is large and it seemed to me it could hold many figures.

Question: Are not the decorations which you painters are accustomed to add to paintings supposed to be suitable and proper to the subject—or are they for pleasure—simply what comes into your imagination?

(A good question, that received a magnificent answer.)

Answer: I paint pictures as I see fit and as well as my talent permits.

Veronese went unpunished, although he cautiously changed the title of the work from "Last Supper" to "Feast at the House of Levi".

Venice protected and inspired its artists. It also liberated them. Go to the Scuola di San Rocco and examine the rooms that Veronese's only rival, Tintoretto, painted. Here in these vast, crowded canvases was the first artist who painted just as he pleased. Study the great, slashing strokes, the wilful compositions, the careless mastery of every technique of painting, and you will see that Venice had brought a new freedom into the world—the freedom that has in our own time given rise to the painters who exhibited at the Bienniale, think of them as you will.

An Added Attraction—the Tourists

Behind the balustrade of the Basilica of St. Mark, tourists listen to an audio machine that dispenses information in Italian, English, French and German.

Venice was a tourist attraction long before the days of guide-books, cameras, postcards and plastic souvenirs. The city had special police to inspect hotels as early as the 13th Century, and a medieval monk recorded, somewhat uncharitably, that "the piazza of St. Mark's seems perpetually filled with Turks, Libyans, Parthians and other monsters of the sea". Today Venice receives nearly two million foreign travellers every year.

And from dawn to dusk, all through the sparkling summer days, they still throng St. Mark's Square. Trailing in ragged regiments behind their voluble guides, they tramp endlessly through sumptuous palaces and churches. In convoys of gondolas they swish along shadowy waterways with crumbling walls. Their numbers increase each year, for the magical decadence of Venice remains just as alluring as ever.

With her guide-book clasped in both gloved
hands, a German visitor in St. Mark's Square,
dressed as if for a garden party, peers up through
sunglasses at the 325-foot bell tower, or
Campanile, the tallest structure in Venice.

A patriotically clad American trains her
camera with intense concentration on the clock
in St. Mark's Square, waiting for the moment
when two mechanical bronze figures of Moors
raise their hammers and strike the hour.

Helped by arm-waving histrionics and folded red umbrella, a guide briefs the large group gathering around her.

With her follow-me umbrella aloft to prevent anyone getting lost in the crowds, the guide leads her straggling party past the loggia of the Doges' Palace.

The art of successful sightseeing is to be
prepared, as demonstrated by this German
group stepping out briskly from the Loggetta at
the base of the Campanile in St. Mark's Square.
Wrapped in their look-alike plastic raincoats,
they are prepared for showers—and for
losing sight of one another in the crowd.

With his camera casually slung over one shoulder and his souvenirs already beginning to mount up, a round-faced visiting youngster on a school tour manages a nicely detached air as he surveys the Venetian scene from under the brim of his rakish hat.

Exhausted by sightseeing, a mixed group of tourists from many different countries sprawls around the steps of a flagpole in St. Mark's Square. Some take time off to write the obligatory postcards home. Others simply relax in the sunshine and watch the Venetians go by.

The end of the visit comes when the tourists' suitcases are piled on to a vaporetto, or water bus, outside a hotel and ferried out under the footbridge to a ship anchored in the Canale di San Marco. Tomorrow there will be new arrivals to take their place, for Venice in all its years has never failed to attract visitors.

7

A Faded Splendour

The more I see of Venice, the more I wonder if there is not something to be said in favour of those Worthy Ones, the Doges and the other men of wealth and power, who ruled the city for so long. After all, everything we see today is of their doing. Now that the extravagances of the Lido are over, no doubt forever, we would not go to see Venice except for the things that they left behind them and which, however reluctantly, they paid good money for.

I was considering this, one glittering morning beside the Grand Canal; and, so thinking, I walked in an abstracted manner into backstage Venice. I did not get lost because I had no particular destination, but I probably looked as lost as a child. A Venetian workman stopped in front of me and said something to which, still deep in compiling my brief for The Worthy Ones, I did not reply. So he said, politely, "*Zanipolo?*"

I nodded. He waved a hand and, in Venetian, said I was almost there. Now, the real name of the square in which, after a step or two, I found myself, is Campo San Giovanni and San Paolo. This, in Venetian, becomes "Zanipolo". Practically every other name in Venice is equally distorted or, as the Venetian prefers to say, made "easier to pronounce". I shall stop, however, at this one instance. It will suffice to show what a long time it takes to understand, much less know, the Venetians, and how dubious are the books written about Venice by foreigners who do not even know Italian correctly. In the square there is a famous statue of a rider on horseback. The celebrated, mellifluous, but pig-headed art critic John Ruskin, for once expressing an opinion with which everybody could agree, wrote, "I do not believe that there is a more glorious work of sculpture existing in the world." I suppose everybody has seen a picture of it, a proud horse ridden by an even prouder rider—a great, swaggering gesture in marvellously wrought bronze.

Every other time I have seen it I have been irritated by the fact that it has been put in a rather poky square, dominated by a brickwork church, and faces towards an open-air restaurant. The Worthy Ones could, I felt, have done better.

But now I was on their side, or trying to be, like a good defence lawyer. I took a seat in the restaurant and recalled the facts. The statue is of Bartolomeo Colleoni, a 15th-Century mercenary leader of troops who fought for pay, and for any side that paid the most. Such men (called *condottieri*) were never heroic figures. Heroism in a leader is a nuisance in any war, but for a commander of mercenaries it would have been downright

This trompe-l'oeil painting by Paolo Veronese (c. 1528-1588) is so realistic that a little girl appears to be peeping round a door in the Villa Barbaro on the Venetian mainland. The painting, in which the only real structural elements are the door frame and the cornice, gave a third dimension to an otherwise blank wall.

foolish; it could easily have led to a wicked waste of his capital, which consisted of his soldiers. Andrea del Verrocchio, the sculptor, has, however, made his *condottiere* the epitome of martial heroism—beetling brows, a hooked nose, and firm lips. His very glance, even in bronze, strikes terror. We are undoubtedly fortunate that Verrocchio never saw his hero but made the whole thing up, having been commissioned to erect the statue after the hero's death. Perhaps all public statues of statesmen and generals would be greatly improved if they were made after the fact and on the same principle.

In any case, the Signoria (the ruling group of The Worthy Ones) were not greatly interested in the warrior. What they wanted was a spanking fine horse. They had the money. Colleoni had left it to them in his will, on condition that they set up a statue to him in St. Mark's Square. The first point in favour of The Worthy Ones is that they refused to do this. Not only would monuments clutter the square, but the horse would detract from the four others from Byzantium on the porch of the church. Their decision showed taste. They read the will and decided that it left them free to put the statue where it now is—in the little square. This verdict showed ingenuity too, but of what sort I cannot say; as they did on innumerable other matters, they kept their reasoning to themselves.

Verrocchio made a superb model of the horse. The Signoria liked it, but decided (again mysteriously) to give the work of producing the rider to another sculptor. Verrocchio lost his temper, smashed the head off the horse and left Venice in a huff. The Signoria, in turn lost their tempers and warned Verrocchio never to set foot in Venice again, at peril of his life.

Verrocchio replied by letter that he had not the slightest intention of coming back to Venice. He pointed out that if the Signoria cut off *his* head, they could not replace it with another. He, Verrocchio, could, on the other hand, easily make another head for the horse and, he added with guile, he could make it *even* better.

The rich merchants were amused. There was no doubt that Verrocchio's horse was a magnificent beast, and here was the master offering to do one better—and not incidentally, pushing up the price to soothe his wounded feelings. They invited him to come back to Venice, promised him that they valued his head *every* bit as much as he did himself, and told him to get on with the statue. They even let him sculpt the rider. Verrocchio died before the statue was completed, but another sculptor finished the work (and impudently wrote his name on the horse's girth). And so, in 1496, The Worthy Ones unveiled an immortal masterpiece.

Sitting in the square and looking at the statue, I reflected that I am often unfair to rich men when they become patrons of something rather above money-grubbing. It was a very hot day and perhaps it was the sun that took my mind back to an experience in tropical Singapore. An immensely wealthy Chinese had invited me to luncheon. Afterwards he took me

In 1479, Venice commissioned an outsider, Florentine sculptor Andrea Verrocchio, to create this monument to Bartolomeo Colleoni, a Venetian mercenary general. The result stunned Venetians with its realism and remains to this day a standard of excellence for equestrian art.

round to his famous collection of orchids; thirty thousand of them, if my memory holds, and mostly growing in the open air. The tour was fascinating to me, but I did not for one moment think that my host really knew anything about orchids: I fancied he clapped his hands one day and said, "I shall have the finest collection of orchids in the world", and lo! there were the thirty thousand. But I was quite wrong. I learned later from his friends, that he knew everything about orchids, although, being Chinese, he had been much too courteous to lecture me. I now suspect he knew what I was thinking.

With these charitable thoughts about the rich in mind, I was determined to take a trip that is always recommended to people who obstinately stay in Venice, but which I had always avoided.

On the other side of the lagoon on which the city is built, lies obviously the mainland. Driving straight north from the lagoon is a canal called the Brenta. Now, the Brenta has become, over the years, one of those phrases that people drop at chic cocktail parties when the topic of Venice arises. You have learned already that the smart reference used to be to "the Lido". After the collapse of that institution, a trip up the Brenta took its place. To have done it showed that you were no ordinary tourist who was satisfied with a ride in a gondola and with buying Venetian glass at the factory in Murano.

A trip up the Brenta meant, in perhaps harsh words, sticking your nose into other people's houses—houses that were far too big to live in comfortably and far too expensive for their long dead (or ruined) owners to keep up—the celebrated "Brenta villas". It was not an expedition that, hitherto, had ever appealed to me. But I had taken up my defence brief for the rich and I therefore decided to make the expedition.

First, however, a word about semantics. It would appear to me that everybody outside Italy thinks that "villa" means "a house"—probably a nice, large house. It does not. From the time of the enormously wealthy ancient Romans it has meant "a farm". Rich Romans kept farms as hobbies, as do rich men today. They went to these farms when Rome grew too hot or, when there was a change of rulers, too dangerous. Cicero was on his way to his "villa" when the executioners caught up with him on the Appian Way. He obligingly stuck his head out between the curtains of his litter and the soldiers equally obligingly cut it off at a stroke.

Rome fell, the centuries rolled on, but the notion that when you had made your pile you bought yourself a farm in the country—a "villa"—survived. The ancient Romans went far afield for their properties. The Venetians, as we might expect, were more cautious. By the 16th Century The Worthy Ones had begun to deceive themselves into thinking that they were really Romans, and some even claimed descent from the ancient families. This was nonsense: no family in Italy, whether in Rome or

The opulent life led by wealthy Venetian aristocrats of the 16th Century can be conjured up by this interior view of the great hall in the Villa Caldogno, a "country house" near Vicenza on the mainland. It was designed by Palladio, the Paduan architect whose innovative principle it was that practical homes could also be luxurious to live in.

Florence or Venice, could trace their genealogy so far back. But they had enough money to buy their "villas", and so they did. They went no farther than the Brenta. The countryside was not (and *is* not) very attractive, but living on the banks of the canal had the advantage that, if bad news arrived from the Rialto, a businessman could get back to Venice quickly in a fast rowing-boat with stalwart oarsmen.

Having a farm usually means a farmhouse, but those are uncomfortable and smelly places. So the rich built themselves houses. It would be wrong to say that they were built in the style to which their owners were accustomed. They lived, the year round, in Venetian palaces; and these, as we have learned, were highly inconvenient. They wanted something more commodious. They got it, and, in getting it, altered the style of domestic architecture for the rich all over the Western world—even, strange as it may seem, America. Everybody who has seen the film "Gone with the Wind" (and who has not?) will have a picture in his mind's eye of the houses we are going to see.

A major point in my brief for the rich Venetians is that, whenever they had need of an original (but not too original) talent, they found one. Just so with the villas. Andrea Palladio (1508-1580) was born in Padua. He soon went to Venice, complete with the idea of what those country houses should look like. They should have style. Indeed, everything the rich did was with style. For their trips to their estates they had specially decorated boats on which they embarked their guests, their cooks, their servants and an orchestra. In these craft they rowed the short distance across the lagoon and into the Brenta, catching the cool breezes.

Palladio realized that the farming side of this foible of his rich patrons was not to be taken too seriously. Thus he separated the work-a-day premises from the house. As for the house itself, he came up with a solution that, simple as it was, appealed greatly to The Worthy Ones. Each room, he said, should be of a size and shape exactly adapted to its purpose. A bedroom should feel like a bedroom; a reception room should be designed to receive. To those used to living in Venice, this was a blessing. As Goldoni has shown us, nobody knew which room in a palazzo was meant for what. From then on, Palladio could do no wrong.

Venetians today still take their boats up the Brenta, and in a style that— our own times being what they are—you must expect. The villas of the Brenta can indeed be visited by road, and I have done it only to find the villas closed, with the custodians away at the local bar much the worse for the local wine. The Brenta is now fully geared for organized tourism, and we can understand why. The modern Venetians have sunk much capital in their boats, and they would not be Venetians if they did not protect their investment.

Petrol engines replace the rowers: piped music plays instead of the orchestra, and there is a snack-bar. ("Snack": the modern Italian is very fond of the word and over the years he has even learned not to spell it "snak".) Do not despise the snack-bar; it is a place of refuge from the guide who, in four languages (and his or her highly individual version of the pronunciation) will pour information at you. We must be tolerant.

The first house is Palladio's masterpiece. It rises high and proudly above the surrounding countryside, with a great columned portico. It is called "La Malcontenta"—the dissatisfied one, the "La" suggesting that the dissatisfied person was a woman. Why? The guide will explain in all four of his languages, giving reasons as wrong as his grammar. It is named, he declares, after a woman belonging to one of the great Venetian families, who locked her up there as a punishment. In unromantic fact it got its name from the local farmers, who had, long before, risen in anger against a near-by property development they did not like—over which they were "malcontent". The name first came to be applied to the area and eventually the house.

But all this is tourist stuff (or perhaps I should say, tourist stuffing). What matters is that, once we are inside La Malcontenta, our feelings are the very reverse of its name. The rooms of various sizes open off the great central hall in a logical sequence, an arrangement that instantly strikes us as right; if you are to build, this of course is the way to do it.

I do not mean that this seems to us an ideal home. Homes are a matter of caprice. We may prefer to live in a New York penthouse, a Jacobean manor-house, a ranch, a cottage in Sussex, or a sun-drenched house in the Caribbean. La Malcontenta has a wider appeal. This building would do for anything—a museum, a court of justice, an embassy, or the residence of some age-old and distinguished clan. It is big, but we do not feel small; it is dignified, but not snobbish. Our eyes run over its proportions with that sense of "just-so, and not otherwise" that one's ears feel in listening to a Bach fugue. We are not surprised that, once seen, Palladio's style was copied all over the world.

This thought brings us back to the device of the portico, with its noble columns. It reminds us of those American mansions of the Deep South, or of those English houses called "stately homes"—as well it might. For Palladio was the inspiration for them. Curiously enough, they are the result of his mistake.

In Palladio's generation, and for long afterwards, everything the ancient Romans had done in the way of art and architecture was considered perfection. Where Palladio's passion and talent for building became apparent, patrons smoothed his path, as was the way in those days, and sent him to Rome, which was full of ruins of the Classical Age. Artists and architects studied them with care, measuring them with foot-rules. They were in a hurry—the same sort of haste that a modern archaeologist feels when some relic of the past has been uncovered by bulldozers that are preparing the ground for a motorway or an office block; he fears that the find will soon disappear forever. So it was with Rome. The Renaissance Popes had determined to make the heart of Christendom the most monumentally impressive city on earth. They succeeded; it is. But unfortunately the Popes were always running out of money. They therefore cannibalized the classic ruins, taking away stones and columns quite freely. The façade of St. Peter's, which television has made the most familiar church-front in history, displays some of their loot.

Palladio was looking for the sort of house a Roman noble might have lived in. Unfortunately, none was left in Rome. Judging from the number of columns he saw lying on the ground (or being dragged away to St. Peter's), he decided that Roman houses must have had great porticos for their entrances and columns all along the front and side, either in the form of whole, round pillars or pilasters with decorated heads.

We know now that he was wrong. The Romans, save for a fortunate few, lived in crowded blocks of flats, some of them six storeys high, so valuable was the land. But we have found their villas out in the country and we know that, from the outside, these buildings had few architectural pretensions. Some must have looked little better than do barracks. The columns were all inside, around pleasant gardens or along cool and shady walks—the original "portico".

It did not matter. The way Palladio used the portico in his designs appealed to every man with money—first in Venice, then in all Italy, later still in Europe, and last of all in America. In addition to those Southern mansions, the Capitol in Washington, D.C., is in the Palladian style, as are many of its imitations in the various states. So is that most beautiful house, Thomas Jefferson's Monticello. The Tsars of Russia built Tsarskoye Selo, according to Palladio's principles; and the English, when they made more money by trade than even the Venetians, went overboard for him. The great English houses of Holkham, Prior Park, Stowe and many others owe their merits to those villas along the Brenta. One more favourable point, then, in my brief for The Worthy Ones.

There was one fault in Palladio's otherwise perfect architecture. It left a lot of blank spaces, blank walls, blank areas over doorways, blank ceilings, and blank interiors of domes. Such voids have always worried designers. In the Middle Ages, architects used stained glass to relieve the emptiness of the wall. As for the roofs, they fretted them with intricate voluting that came to resemble the over-arching branches of trees in a forest. But this was too frivolous for the Roman style espoused by Palladio.

Again and again the houses on the Brenta show the solution. The Venetians had expert painters. They set them to covering the walls and the domes and any other space with frescos. Michelangelo had shown what could be done with the dull roof of the Sistine Chapel in the Vatican. The Venetian painters—ready, as always, to decorate anything for a fee —set to work with a will.

Palladio's villa La Malcontenta overlooks the Brenta. It was commissioned by the Foscari family, whose lands lay only a short boat ride from Venice. The drawings of the villa's plans and elevation (below) were published in 1570 by Palladio, one of the most influential architectural theorists of his day, as part of a comprehensive text-book devoted to his building method.

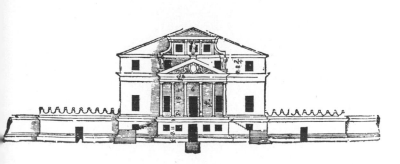

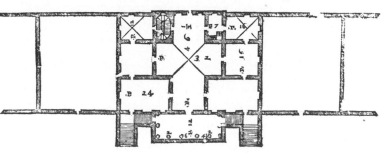

We have only to look around us to see with just how much of a will. The largest of the houses is that built by the Pisani family, more than a century after Palladio but still dominated by his style. The bare places are covered with an astonishing display of the painters' art, especially their skill in deceiving the eye. Perspective has been so mastered that when we think we see columns they turn out to be pictures of columns; corridors lead away from a room where there are no corridors at all. The ceiling of the great central hall, which was used as a ballroom, has disappeared behind invisible glass (or so it seems); we look up instead into a heaven, a sky crowded in the Venetian manner, with figures celebrating the triumph of the family that paid for the house—all of them seen as we earth-bound plebeians would really see them, if that heaven were real.

We are looking at the last, bold, desperate gesture of The Worthy Ones, before darkness and decay closed in upon the beautiful city they had made. And at this point I must come to the most difficult part of our journey together. We have been puzzled, critical, admiring and, finally, under-standing about Venice. It has taught us, as few other places in the world can do, to use our eyes. Now we must use them again, less happily.

As we troop in and out of the houses on the Brenta, one thing cannot escape our well-trained eyes. The houses are dilapidated. Stucco was an invention of the Palladian period. It consists of ground-up stone mixed with a binding agent. It was supposed to last as long as real stone, but it does not. The houses show it. Every blow registers on it, as it does on the face of an aging pugilist, and the mark does not go away. It can be patched, but the patches show.

Frescos, too, fade, and they can peel away from the wall. Damp is a problem that has never been wholly solved on the Italian peninsula and is only partially solved today with techniques that cost an enormous amount of money. As we walk through the houses of the Brenta, this damp eats into us and makes patterns on the wall that no artist ever intended.

These great houses were used only during the summer. If the weather turned chilly, they were heated by braziers. Besides, their occupants were clothed in layer after layer of wool, to say nothing of thick-soled boots to keep out the chill of the marble floors. I speak with knowledge—and feeling. I once visited regularly an aging *principessa* in her Renaissance palace in Venice, first to listen to her reminiscences, secondly to study her magnificent surroundings. Her palace, too, was heated only by these braziers and, whenever I went to sip sweet liqueurs with her, I put on woollen underclothing. The houses on the Brenta were finally deserted when the damp had its way.

The gardens today are wildernesses. Broken statues adorn their walks; moss and weeds occupy the once-smooth paths. Summer pavilions have shutters that flap mournfully in the wind, while rain trickles through the roofs and eats away what is left of the painted decorations.

It could have been worse. The impoverished owners of these houses might well have stripped off the roofs before moving away in order to avoid paying taxes. But the English came to the rescue. I have noted that the builders of the country houses of England were enamoured of Palladio and his style. It followed that, when the English began to visit Italy in droves after the Second World War, they wanted to see the stately homes that had started the whole affair. Very reluctantly, the Venetians saw—puzzling as it was—that they had another source of tourist income. Many of the houses were therefore saved from actual ruin, but not with any great enthusiasm. The houses on the Brenta had long ago been stripped of everything movable, the contents sold. Now, they were sparsely furnished anew. The result is that the houses look as though they have been visited by bailiffs.

As the years went on, however, the English tourists grew poorer, and therefore more rare. The Italians themselves were more concerned with the healthier habit of driving down their new six-lane motorways than visiting the mouldering houses of an extinct aristocracy. But then came a sensation. Venice—the real Venice, the city itself—was in danger, it was said, of sinking into the sea. Or, if that was a little far-fetched, then certainly it was in peril of dropping bit by bit into the canals. As along the Brenta, the palaces on the Grand Canal were falling into disrepair and there was no money to put them right. The statues on the churches were being eaten away by noxious fumes from the motor boats and the factories on the mainland. The waves caused by the propellers of the big ships in the lagoon were shaking the whole foundation of the city. Artesian wells, supplying water to a population that was increasingly concerned with personal hygiene (and to tourists, in ever-growing numbers) had lowered the "water-table" of the town. Suddenly the cry went up, "Can it all be saved?"

The Seagirt Satellites

Seen from San Lazzaro, an island inhabited by Armenian monks (the poles hold their fishing nets), the late sun lays a golden path across the slate-grey lagoon.

The city of Venice actually extends much farther than the dolphin-shaped cluster of islands around the Grand Canal. Its boundaries embrace all the other islands scattered across the lagoon and the near-by mainland shores. Within this area are dozens of distinct communities, some with histories stretching back farther than that of the Doges. They include industrial centres, fishing ports, housing developments and playgrounds for the rich. A few of the islands are populous towns; some are farms; others have become refuges for seclusion-seeking monks or conveniently isolated sites for tuberculosis and psychiatric hospitals. The water that separates them also binds them together. Most can be reached by ferry or motor-launch services and none is more than two hours from Venice proper, which sits in their midst, a queen among her subjects.

Dense ranks of changing-huts and sunshades, strewn with drying towels and bathing suits, line the beach of Venice's famous Lido, a narrow strip of land between the lagoon and the Adriatic. Once an island of sand dunes and market gardens, the Lido is now crowded with hotels, private houses, cars and buses.

Because of its narrow lanes and its tiny houses that shine in the bright, primary colours of a child's painting, Burano has been likened to a toy village. While over the centuries other islands have boomed and faded back to wasteland, Burano has remained a stable community, living on fishing and lacemaking.

The cypresses of San Michele, which has been Venice's cemetery since Napoleon decreed that the dead were to be buried there, stand above the island's graves like a gathering of mist-shrouded mourners. Because of a lack of space, bones must be dug up after a dozen or so years and deposited in an ossuary.

The quayside of Chioggia, one of the busiest fishing ports on the Adriatic, is a floating thicket of masts and booms. The town, on two islands near the lagoon's southern end, was founded before Venice and, even when ruled by the city, was still allowed to have its own Grand Chancellor, a unique concession by the Doges.

Regularly dredged channels criss-cross a heavily silted portion of the Venetian lagoon where houses—with characteristic Venetian chimney pots—stand isolated from one another. In the past, silt from rivers emptying into the lagoon threatened to change it into a dry delta. As a result of the process, and of tide-borne sand, most of its 64 square miles now are shallows.

Steering towards posts that mark channel limits for vessels of deeper draughts, boatmen approach the mainland petrochemical and port complex of Marghera in the half-lit gloom of a lagoon evening. The squat gas tanks in front of them stand in starkest contrast to the elegant architecture of the city they serve.

8

Surviving the Present

Once word got around that Venice and all its treasures were in danger of being lost, international committees were formed to raise funds. Art historians were summoned to meetings with engineers, environmental experts, and a whole host of university professors who were nothing loath to mourn over Venice with expenses paid. The expected submergence of Venice eclipsed for a while even the threatened population explosion of the Third World as a topic of earnest and undoubtedly high-minded conversation throughout the West.

The only people who were not worked up about it were the Venetians. For one thing, they owned the place. A person who actually owns an ancient monument has a quite different attitude towards it than the rest of us do. He, his father, his grandfather, his great-grandfather, all always had known that the place might fall down and they had spent their lives in incessant repairs. They had also dealt with relays of architects who had long ago told them the truth: any building, however well put up, needs a thorough overhaul every 200 years. As for foundations, Venice might be built on mud, but many other cities are built on substrata that pose similar problems. The English, who were the most alarmed at the fate of Venice, could well look to their own cathedrals. Within 200 years of having been put up, no fewer than 11 had disastrous collapses, and the rest have been in trouble ever since.

But I shall let a Venetian speak for himself. He owns an ancient building just off the Grand Canal. He revealed to me what I have just recorded, but he also told me more. Going round the galleries and churches with me, and helping me through the maze of Venetian art, he had said, regarding the crumbling façade of a particularly dilapidated palace:

"I am convinced that all those good Americans and English and Germans are right. They always convince me in the end. We Italians do not take proper care of our heritage. I thought that the Americans and English were wrong when they destroyed Monte Cassino by bombing. I thought they were wrong when they shattered whole areas of Florence. I thought they were wrong when they smashed up part of Rome even when it was an open city. But, of course, I was mistaken. I was just a stupid dilettante who could not see further than my nose. It was war, and it had to be done. And, of course, everybody was quite right when they bombed Venice, although—stupidity again—I did not think so at the time. Ah, yes, indeed; we need you foreigners to teach us how to preserve these marvels of the past of which we Venetians are such careless custodians."

Seen under the beetling bow of another huge anchored vessel, an oil tanker as big as a cathedral lies moored off the island of Poveglia in the quiet waters of the Venetian lagoon. The volume of modern shipping and the deep-channel dredging required for the gigantic ships are among the reasons given for the pollution and flooding that threaten to destroy Venice.

But that, of course, is only a sarcastic old Venetian talking, a descendant of The Worthy Ones who now has to rent out his house as lodgings. He is the descendant, too, of those other Venetians who, when the great bell-tower of St. Mark's fell down one day in 1902, built it up again, brick by brick, in ten short years—and out of their own pockets.

Why are the Venetians so indifferent? Why do they arrange receptions for visiting experts in their insanitary palaces, and then go off by themselves in the corners of their great reception halls and talk local gossip? Because it is all over. The Venetians are like the offspring of geniuses. They proudly bear a famous name, but in their heart of hearts it is like a weight of lead upon their shoulders. That becomes very clear when, as I have done, one goes into their libraries. The archives are there, great dusty bundles of them. They are open to anyone who takes the trouble to untie the tapes. But there is no great Venetian historian who has gone through them and spent his life writing a masterpiece on the many riches they contain. There is no Venetian Gibbon or Toynbee; not even one to compare to those lesser names who, elsewhere, seem to have dug into the past of their countries down to the least detail. The rest of Italy has produced great critics of art—Benedetto Croce, Adolfo Venturi and others. But Venice has been content to leave the matter to an American who lived and died in Florence: Bernard Berenson.

Only on one day of the year do the Venetians remember their past. On the third Sunday of July, a festival is held. It is for themselves alone; tourists are forgotten and will find little to entertain them if they choose to go. For myself, I find attendance moving, but then I have a passion for ruins and dead cities. Not that this festival is held in a tomb-like silence; on the contrary, the noise and the music can be deafening. But, to me, there is an air of ghosts at the revels. In the 16th Century a great plague of typhus struck Venice. If we can take our eyes away from the pictures in the Scuola di San Rocco, we can also find there a contemporary inscription that tells the story: "In 1576, when Mocenigo was Doge, a contagious pestilence flared up. None ever lasted longer; none ever more destructive. It was a just punishment for our sins."

Fifty thousand Venetians died, and among them were three hundred of the noble ones—the carrier lice, apparently, never having read the "Golden Book". The epidemic ended in the mysterious way that such do. In penitence, The Worthy Ones decided to erect a great church, and Palladio designed it. It is called the Church of the Redentore (the Redeemer) and to see it we must cross the Giudecca Canal to the other bank, which is a long island called the Giudecca. It was once a wooded, green and silent place, so quiet that Michelangelo, in one of his moods, wished to spend the rest of his days there, away from the human race. I need not say that today the island is very crowded. Towering above it is the church—white, austere, but graceful to the eye.

It is the last church that we shall visit together and it immediately reminds us of one of the first. There is a great dome, strangely Byzantine in its lines, like that of St. Mark's. There is another touch of the East; two turrets rise on either side, like the minarets of a mosque.

But, once inside, all is classical, all Palladio. The great public baths of ancient Rome must have looked very much like this, with a great apse and huge columns in stately array. Palladio's sense of proportion is nowhere better shown than here. He himself laid great stress on the fact that he had worked to fixed mathematical rules. No doubt he did, but his measuring rods were held by inspired hands. His arithmetical calculations are of interest only to architects, who always modestly claim that they are merely practical men solving practical problems in a practical way. The Redentore, for us, is not an exercise in mathematics, but a cool, serene and noble place, a pinnacle in the story of art.

On the day of the festival, Venetians come to this church, sometimes travelling from afar. It is proper to come by water. Anybody who has a boat —be it a launch, a gondola, or a skiff—piles into it and crosses the Giudecca Canal. After the mass, they stay in their boats, singing, drinking and eating (the ritual dish is mulberries). They rejoice all night and then go over to the Lido to see the sunrise. Their procession is the last and the only genuine survivor of the great and splendid marches of the past.

So far we have been concerned with the past of Venice, with an excursion or two into the present. But what of the future? I admit that in my previous visits to Venice, from boyhood onwards, I had not given that future a thought. The Venetians with whom I usually spent my time were all elderly scholars, the remnants of the aristocracy; well-heeled people with long memories and the art of reminiscence. But on the visit I paid before I sat down to write this book, I spent some time on a different inquiry. I spoke to the young people.

Foreigners whose image of the Italians comes from books, or films about the Mafia, or tales of bottom-pinching Latin lovers, are often very disappointed with the young Venetians. They shrug them off as dull. A word of explanation is in order.

After speaking so much of doges and Titian and Veronese, it will come, I am sure, as an anticlimax if I go on to talk of television; but it is necessary. When Mussolini set out to rule Italy (and not least, the proud and independent Venetians), he promulgated a law that forbade anybody from leaving the province in which he was born to seek work elsewhere—unless that person had special permission, which was difficult to get. He believed it was the heart of the Italian character to be bound, emotionally, to where his family lived. *Paese*—which means your native countryside, or town, or even village—was a word carried all over the world by Italian emigrants; and *paesano* became a term of recognition, and greeting whenever two

Across the lagoon—beyond the rooftops, television aerials and graceful campaniles of the old city—the chimneys of Marghera, Venice's industrial complex, corrupt a golden evening haze. From such chimneys come the corrosive pollutants that are eating into Venice's ancient stonework.

Italians from the same place met. Mussolini, who always claimed to be right, was not in this instance as wrong as was his usual habit. There was a great deal of truth in his concept. Even as late as the early Fifties, Italians from Turin would tell me that the Neapolitans, or Sicilians, or the locals wherever I was living at the time were not really Italians; while the Neapolitans would say, in disgust, that the people in Turin were really French. None of the parties, of course, knew much about any of the others. If they travelled on holiday, they spent hours at café tables writing post-cards home to *La Mamma*, saying how much they longed to be back with her. The Venetians were foremost in this nostalgia for the *paese*.

Then, in the Fifties, came television, and I witnessed its impact. After an initial attempt to feed the public on a diet of opera, bicycle-racing, football and political discussions, the authorities threw open the windows. Italy and the world poured into the family living-room, as it has done elsewhere, but with a much greater effect because Mussolini's law no longer applied.

Italians began to see how other Italians lived, particularly those who were making piles of money in the manufacturing towns of the North, such as Milan and Turin. A vast movement of the population took place from poorer to richer areas, and it is still going on. When I first went to live in Italy, after the Second World War, a standard joke was told of the lad who was on his knees making his confession. He mentioned that he had been to Rome and the village priest was supposed to have asked, as if to a sinner, "How many times, my son, how many times?" By the time, not so long ago, when a million people turned up in Rome from every province of Italy to follow the funeral of the Communist leader, Togliatti, that joke would have become incomprehensible. On this visit I talked to the sons of the Venetians I had known. I sat in at their discussions, which were not about Titian or Veronese, or even about sinking into the sea. They talked about jobs and housing and social security, and the way politicians broke their promises. They talked, in a word, like the young all over the world. Venice, the beautiful Venice of which their fathers and forefathers had been so proud, was never mentioned at all. Their interest centred around a town as different from Venice as can be imagined. It is called Marghera, and anyone who is anxious about the drowning of Venice should visit it, because Marghera is largely to blame. If you go by road you may well pass through it—an added reason for going by boat. Marghera is a huge indus-trial complex, three times bigger than Venice. It is also a port like Venice, but four times as busy. It is thriving; it is where the young work. The great petrol carriers that use its port churn up the waters of the lagoon and shake Venice to its foundations. But whatever happens to the old city, Marghera will continue to expand.

To the foot-weary tourist, Marghera is something of a relief; there is nothing whatever to see, except factories. There is, indeed, one large modern church that even has a mosaic. But the less said about either the

On the island of Torcello a cartouche on a crumbling garden wall displays an eagle's winged foot, the crest of the ancient Malipiero family who once had a palace there. One of the first lagoon islands to be settled, Torcello originally outshone Venice herself, but gradually fell into decay.

better. However, if you need packaged food, chemicals, electrical goods, steel, cloth, or building materials, Marghera is the place to go. The younger generation are proud of it. Their ancestors, like Marco Polo, had to journey to the Far East to make their fortunes; the modern Venetian has merely to cross the lagoon to stand a chance of getting comparatively rich too. Most do not want to make even that short, two-and-a-half mile voyage. The ambition of every young married couple is to live in one of the new blocks of flats in Marghera or in near-by Mestre, where they can surround themselves with all the things they see nightly in the advertisements on television; and these, I hardly need to say, are not gondolas or frescos or paintings or mathematically perfect churches. So, for the young, the future of Venice is Marghera. How right are they? What other future is there for them? It so happens that we can get, with ease, a vivid picture of the alternative.

I will put aside tourism. For one thing it employs far fewer people than the tourist imagines. For another, not everybody wants to be in service to other people. Thomas Jefferson, after making an extensive tour of Europe in the 1780s, made a remark to the effect that it is unwise to judge a people by their ostlers. Ostlers, of course, were men who took care of horses at an inn, rather like the bellboys who take care of us in hotels today. Tourism calls for a certain sort of person and in these days, when the dignity of labour is exalted above the dignity of doges, the young are unwilling even to be bellboys.

But by something of a miracle, the sort of life the young Venetian might have had to lead, had there been no Marghera, still survives. Although the young abhor Venice, to us—not born or bound to it—a visit to the city has a peaceful charm.

So far, we have seen three Venices. The first was the one that surrounds the Grand Canal: the Venice of palaces, great churches and masterpieces. Next, we have seen backstage Venice, the mesh of little canals, tiny bridges, markets and slums. This is the Venice where the inhabitants, of an evening, no longer lean out of their windows to watch one another or the passers-by below, but stay at home to gaze at the flickering electronic image of a cleaner, wider world that does not smell so bad. And in our mind's eye we have seen a Venice that has disappeared—a rich, pleasure-loving town of theatres and grand parties; a Venice of easy morals, *cicisbei*, and foreigners kicking up their heels and writing poetry. There is yet another Venice. It has no palaces, and if it has churches I promise you we shall not go into them. But this last Venice has one supreme virtue. It is quiet. It is empty. If it has tourists, they are not many; and they are all gone by dusk. It is the sort of place that Michelangelo yearned for and that the Venetian of today does his best to forget.

There are other islands in the lagoon besides the Lido and the Giudecca. They are perhaps the most refreshing things to be seen in

Outside her doorway, an elderly lacemaker reproduces the intricacies of an 18th-Century pattern.

Burano's Busy Needles

The island of Burano has been a lace-making centre for four and a half centuries. Its lace, once the most sought-after in the world, has always been made with care: only white human hairs, for example, were fine enough to produce a lace collar for Louis XIV of France. The industry almost died in the 19th Century under competition from cheap, machine-made items. Only one 70-year-old woman still knew the secrets of *punto Buranese*—Burano point—in 1872 when a school was founded to revive the art. Now, while the men fish, the women of Burano ply their needles.

At home or sitting outdoors in barefoot ease, the women rarely put aside their needles and tomboli, the traditional lap cushions on which they work.

Venice. But if the visitor is pressed by anybody in the ostler industry (if I may call it that) to be guided on his tour, he should firmly refuse. The islands should be seen alone; and by people who do not wish to be alone, they should not be seen at all. It is a piece of advice that is good for the soul, as well as a protection for your pocket.

Rove back a moment to where we began. The Venetians fled the mainland because of the onslaught of the barbarians. The history of the times is obscured by flame, smoke and massacre. But peering through it all, it would seem that their first choice of refuge was an island in the lagoon called Torcello.

We arrive at Torcello by ferry. We step ashore and immediately we are in another world. There is water, there are canals, just as in Venice. But the canals are not lined with palaces; their banks are all but deserted. Small two-storeyed houses painted in bright colours extend in a diminishing perspective—one that is inviting, quiet, peaceful. Even the boatmen do not shout as they must do in Venice, to be heard above the motor boats.

Yet this *is* Venice. A tower rises above the roofs of the houses. It leads us to a church, set in a silence like that of an English cathedral. It is the first cathedral of Venice, begun in 639. It is simple in design, clearly put up by a people who counted the cost of every brick. (I will keep my promise; we will not go in). The fortunes of the people who settled here, in houses that could not have been very different from those we see, were derived from the geographical fact that Torcello lay, protected by the marshes, between the golden civilization of Byzantium and the hungry markets of Europe. Here—as witness, hard by the cathedral—is the church of Santa Fosca, perfect in its Byzantine form.

Once, Torcello had dreams of glory. But mosquitoes put an end to them in the 16th Century. Malaria laid low the population and history moved over to other islands, to come to rest in the Venice of today. The people of Torcello are now merely fishermen—concerned, like fishermen the world over, solely with their own affairs. Nor is a visitor, even if he is an Italian from the mainland, likely to find what these affairs are. The Venetian dialect is difficult; the way they speak in Torcello is impossible. The inhabitants sit mending their nets, or at the doors of their dark houses, exchanging comments so incomprehensible that they might be stories of the happenings behind Byzantium walls of triple brass. At least, once you get well away from Torcello's landing-stage and the tourist guides, you have a chance to think so. Unless you seek out the antiquities (and they are few enough), you will be left to yourself, as nowhere else in Italy today except in the heart of Calabria far to the south.

Torcello declined and another island, close by, took over—how or why no one knows for sure. It is called Burano. I believe it to be the most romantically beautiful sight in the whole lagoon. At Burano you must not expect castles, turrets or bosky glades. The island is as flat as a pancake. It has one tower. But it appears to be lit both from the sun and the sea. Its green fields are mirrored in the waters by which you approach—never quite reaching it—like pastures laid out and ready for gatherings of Arcadians, those mythical Greeks who were so happy in their simplicity. Approaching by gondola in a silence broken only by the oars, Burano rises—even more magically than Venice—against its enormous backcloth of the sky.

You land, and that is the end of the enchantment. The houses are like those of Torcello, small and bright. But the women of Burano know how to make lace. They sit in the streets, winding the threads round their pins with fleet, skipping, but gnarled fingers. For centuries they have been making lace and selling it. They still want to sell it; and if you are unwise enough to have gone to Burano with a tourist guide, he will see to it that you buy some. The lace is very expensive—as it should be, since every knot is tied by hand. It will last for generations. It should be bought by anyone who can imagine granddaughters and great-granddaughters well into the 21st Century who will wear lace heirlooms.

Of course, they might. But that does not concern the younger generation of Venice and Marghera. One young man I met in Marghera was born on Burano. What strikes him is that his mother and his sisters and his aunts are the finest makers of lace in the world; they have been making it all their lives and yet they have no motor car. Of course, you may say that a motor car would be of small use to them on a tiny island. Still, it is a nice thing to have; and he has one. That is why he works in Marghera and swears that his children will work there too. They can, he says, go back to Burano—for Christmas and Easter. Not otherwise. And never to make lace.

When, as a lad, I first watched these women at work, my heart was filled with the most generous emotions. To spend one's life at so skilled a profession, to create those beautiful patterns from mere, dull thread—and yet to be so poor: I made a comparison: the factory worker in Detroit, doing no more than endlessly tighten bolts as car-chassis after car-chassis passed by his glazing eye, and yet earning much, much more than these artisans of Burano. It did not seem fair. Such rare skills, I thought, would in a better world be better rewarded. I had fantasies of a liberal-minded doge giving gold coins to these poor, bent women with their lined faces because, through their consummate skill, they honoured Venice.

And, of course, I did buy yards of lace. I gave the lace to my mother, who never throughout her long life, found what to do with it. Nowadays, watching the women at work, I hear instead the contemptuous voice of that young man from Burano making petro-chemicals in Marghera who had said, while he dangled his youngest offspring on his knee, "Anybody can make lace." Well, I suppose anybody can, given patience and a lesson or two. Yet everybody who has spent days wandering through the palaces and churches and squares of Venice must have a question running through

Molten glass has to cool briefly before blowing.

Powerful lungs are needed to use a blowing iron.

Shears are used to cut the rim of a glass bowl.

A craftsman uses a tool to flare the bowl's lip.

A Fiery Art

Glass was a Venetian monopoly, and furnaces like the one on the right have glowed on the island of Murano since they were moved there from Venice in 1291 to protect the city from frequent fires. The maestros of Murano boasted that their goblets were so dainty they shattered if touched by a drop of poison. Venice indulged the maestros in some matters, allowing the islanders their own council and aristocracy and letting them coin their own money. But any glassmaker who dared take his skills elsewhere was tracked down and killed by the city's agents. The trade secrets leaked out anyway, and by 1600 Venetian glass was already being widely copied. But Murano has maestros still.

A blown glass sphere is inserted into the glowing furnace to soften. The glass will then be spun on the rod to flatten it by centrifugal force into a bowl shape.

his mind. All those skills that went into the gilded carvings, the vast frescos, the intricate goldsmith's work of the Pala d'Oro, the glowing mosaics, have they all disappeared?

In the rest of Italy they have not. In the gardens of the Vatican City there is a studio that, if you have the money, will copy any religious painting you choose in mosaic as fine, and perhaps finer, than done in the past. In Florence there is a shop that will bind your books in leather, with tooling as splendid as any library of antique books can show. In Rome, the firm that cast the bells of St. Peter's remains to this day the best caster in bronze in the whole world.

It is not so in Venice. Only one of the crafts for which ancient Venice was renowned is still practised. To see it we must visit the glass-blowers. They work on the island of Murano and it does not matter, this time, if you take a guide or not. The island swarms with them, all proclaiming at the tops of their voices that the visit to the factory is free, quite free, and promising that it is a wonderful show. It is. You are shown into a vast room with containers glowing eerily with molten glass, some of it shining with jewel-like colours. The workmen—at least, those on show—are strapping fellows with broad smiles and even broader chests. Your guide selects one of them for the performance. The craftsman takes up a long, thin tube and dips it into the glass. He twirls it and pulls it out, a large blob of the glass hanging from the end. He then blows down the tube, his cheeks distended like those of the spirits of the Four Winds on old-time maps, his pectoral muscles swelling magnificently. The blob at the end becomes a ball. Playing unheard music on his tube, the craftsman shapes the ball as he will, twiddling the tube, his cheeks going in and out like those of a jazz trumpeter. He takes up a pair of shears, snips here and snips there, twiddles anew, puffs and huffs—and there is a wine-glass. If you prefer a vase, he will make you a vase. It can be in any colour you choose, but you will show connoisseurship if you ask for green. That colour, a rich emerald, is the hall mark of Murano glass. If you would go further and want a vase of your own design, you will be whisked off elsewhere, to place your order. Months later it will be delivered to your house and you will put it on a table, an object to treasure both for its workmanship and for the money you will have paid for it.

If you do not aim so high, you will be taken to a showroom with shelves and tables loaded with glass, blown and twisted into all conceivable shapes. There are goblets in imitation of those the Borgias might have used, chalices chased with exquisite designs, wine-glasses with stems so thin and fragile that they will intimidate your guests, and even little glass animals with quaint expressions that you will either fall in love with or remember as the most horrifically tasteless things you have ever seen. Murano is Venetian, and in Venice the customer has always been right. Thus, unless you have a will of iron and a hide as thick as a rhinoceros, you will buy something before you leave.

The difference between low tide (top) and high tide (bottom) is normally small, but then Venice has little margin for safety. Any tide higher than usual immediately becomes a threat. The building in the foreground is the old customs house; the domed structure across the lagoon is Palladio's Il Redentore, the Church of the Redeemer.

There is also a glass museum that, for me sums up Venice. Nothing else so evokes The Worthy Ones in their glory and extravagance. It begins with items of the Renaissance, among them a cup made specially for a marriage. The shape is as bold and as perfect as a Chinese vase, and it may well have been copied from some Chinese original brought to Venice in the caravans. There is a picture in the cup of the young bridegroom, and pictures that tell in allegory of the joys of marriage. It is an extraordinarily lovely piece of work. Then there are drinking glasses of the period, too precious to be touched here, although I have handled similar ones elsewhere and even carried their smooth rims to my lips.

Then, as you pass along the show-cases, the quality of the glass itself improves until it is as clear as rock-crystal. The craftsmen of Murano had discovered a secret process that caused their wares to be in demand all over Europe. Venice passed stringent laws to guard the secret, even threatening death to anyone who betrayed it.

Yet it was betrayed. The secret passed to Bohemia and glass from central Europe became the best in the world. It could also be bought at much lower prices than the Venetians asked. By the 18th Century Murano had declined, just as Venice itself declined, and the descent of both is clearly recorded. The show-cases became the pages of a history book. Murano was eclipsed because her art passed elsewhere. Venice fell for much the same reason; the trade routes of the world had changed. The ships of Spain and Portugal, of Holland and England replaced the proud flotillas of the Venetians. Venice grew poorer and poorer, and The Worthy Ones more pressed for money. Goldoni, in the play we saw, caught the colours of that sunset. Then came the conquering French, flushed with the triumph of the Revolution. The Doge was deposed, the last of his line. A Tree of Liberty was planted in St. Mark's Square and the bronze horses were carried away. To the discerning eye it is all here, on Murano; the designs grow clumsier and more vulgar, the workmanship worse. The striving to please the taste of the foreign visitors who are now the Venetians' bread and butter is painful to see.

All is not quite lost, however. Murano's workmen do still, almost as a hobby, turn out beautiful things that reflect their famous past. I once bought a clear white vase because its shape struck an echo in my mind, but of what I could not recall. Then, one day, I saw this same vase down in the corner of a huge painting by Veronese. A modern craftsman had seen it too, and copied it. I suppose that vase was the thing I most valued in my house in Rome. If I could never own a Veronese, at least I could have something he had designed—he, or perhaps one of his assistants who was ordered to fill in that corner under the master's eye. The vase lasted until a maidservant knocked it over. As she remarked, it was a stupid thing, no good for flowers because they died too quickly when she put them in its narrow, elegant top.

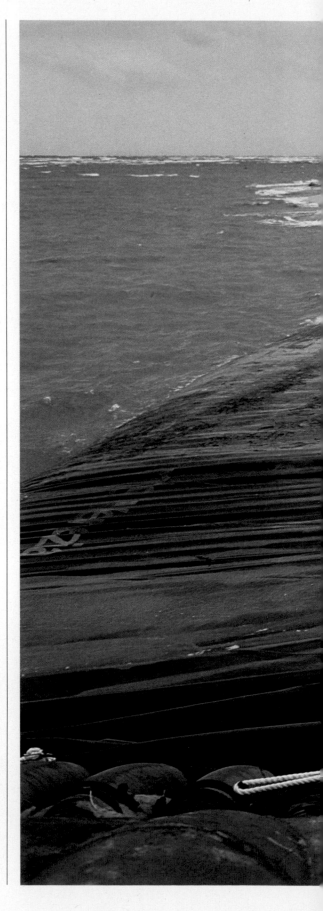

A rubber dam stretches across a narrow channel near Venice; when pumped full of water, it expands and retards the highest tides, so reducing flooding.

I think that my broken vase is a symbol of what the future of Venice will be; the future, I mean, of 10, 20, 30 years hence. I believe that it will be a happy and tranquil one.

My Veronese vase was graceful to the eye but, as my maidservant correctly said, impractical. I accept her judgment. She was working for me only as a stop-gap. Her aim was to find a post in the factories of northern Italy, just as it is the aim of the young Venetians. My vase was not the sort that would in due course, suit her modern arrangements; a colour television, a washing machine, and a car in the communal garage.

Venice, too, will soon become impractical, at least as a place where the rising generation will want to live. So they will leave. Will that mean that Venice will become a dead city? By no means.

We live in a world where, with very little fuss, we can take whole Egyptian temples to pieces and re-erect them on a hill, where they will be safe from the waters of the Aswan Dam; or we can transport them to New York and put them up inside a museum. We live in a world where Art is such a commercial attraction that the interior of the Parthenon in Athens has had to be closed because the feet of the visitors are wearing out the ancient pavement.

When, as I have mentioned, Walt Disney guided me through his land of fantasy, I told him over our lunch that his amusing invention would be copied all over the globe, as kings once copied the Palace of Versailles. It happened, of course. But no one will ever be able to copy Venice and, for that very reason, it will be preserved. The floodwaters will be held back by barriers, the crumbling stone-work of the palaces will be sprayed with preservatives, the broken statues repaired.

Venice will be saved because we live in a world where the town hall of Ypres, totally destroyed in the First World War, has been raised again and few people, unless informed by a guide-book, will notice any difference. We already know that if the roof of the Sistine Chapel were to collapse, we could recreate it photographically. Moreover, we also know that the new roof would not flake away, as the old one does, little by little, each passing year. So, there is nothing we cannot do if there is enough money, and the money will be found.

As for Venice itself, backstage Venice will slowly empty. The ancient buildings will be gutted, leaving only their façades, which—because of the extravagant rents that will be charged for the new offices and for the flats built behind them—will shine in their original glory. I need no experts to tell me this; I have watched it happen in Trastevere, once a slum quarter of Rome, that has become a place where only the rich are able to live.

The noisy motor boats will be banned, or hushed by new devices. The gondoliers will get what they already consider their rights: a subsidy from the State as living historical monuments. They are tired of being piratical. I was happy to be able to tell one of their union organizers how the drivers of Rome's famous horse-drawn carriages won the right, both for themselves and their horses, to be provided with square meals out of Rome's equivalent of City Hall, bankrupt as it is. (He gave me a free ride as a result.) "If", as he said, while propelling his boat, "those lazy, idle Romans can do it, so can we."

There will be a new canal to accommodate the big ships going to Marghera and thus the waves that damage Venice will be eliminated. The poisonous fumes from Marghera's chimneys, which are eating away the stonework of the palaces, will be a thing of the past. There will be no difficulty about controlling such pollution. It was done years ago in London, whose famous fogs—which trapped noxious fumes—can now be seen only in Hollywood movies.

The palaces will be divided into flats, and I think that something of the oriental splendour of old Venice will return when the oil-sheiks—with their flowing robes and golden daggers at their waists—settle in. Seeing them, I did not ask if they were buying property, as they have been in all the other beautiful places of the earth. What Venetian would be so unbusinesslike as to tell me if they were? Venice may change, but not the Venetians.

Thus, in a few years, Venice will be impractical—and beautiful to look at, like my Veronese vase. Its ancient loveliness will return, cared for by millions of lire of public money that would have made even The Worthy Ones green with envy. It will be the city they aimed to make.

But for now let us take one last walk beside the Grand Canal. Let us take a farewell look at Venice before it becomes, as it will, a museum city. Looking about me, I—for one—am not sorry at the prospect. There is nothing wrong with museums—provided, as I have learned, we do not leave our imaginations on the mainland.

The Ephemeral Venice

Quintessentially Venetian in its air of melancholy and decay, a figure of Christ gazes down from a peeling shrine, ignored by a passing child of the present.

Venice is the possession of the whole world. The look of its buildings and canals is just as familiar to the many who have never been there as to the relatively few who have made a perfunctory stop of a day or two. But there is another Venice, visible only to the unhurried visitor to the city and to the islands of its lagoon: views not illustrated in any brochure and not described in any guide-book; sights—fleeting, momentary, unpredictable—not to be found again even if you return the next day for a second look. Depending perhaps on the light, perhaps on an echo of similarity between old and new, such images need the sensitive eye of a constructive observer—or the camera of a photographer—to make the connection, to catch the subliminal reference. Quietly entertaining glimpses like these, however, often linger most vividly in the memory.

A pair of sea boots, unceremoniously up-ended to drain, add a jarring note to a classic Venetian scene: moored gondolas shining with the gloss of recent rain.

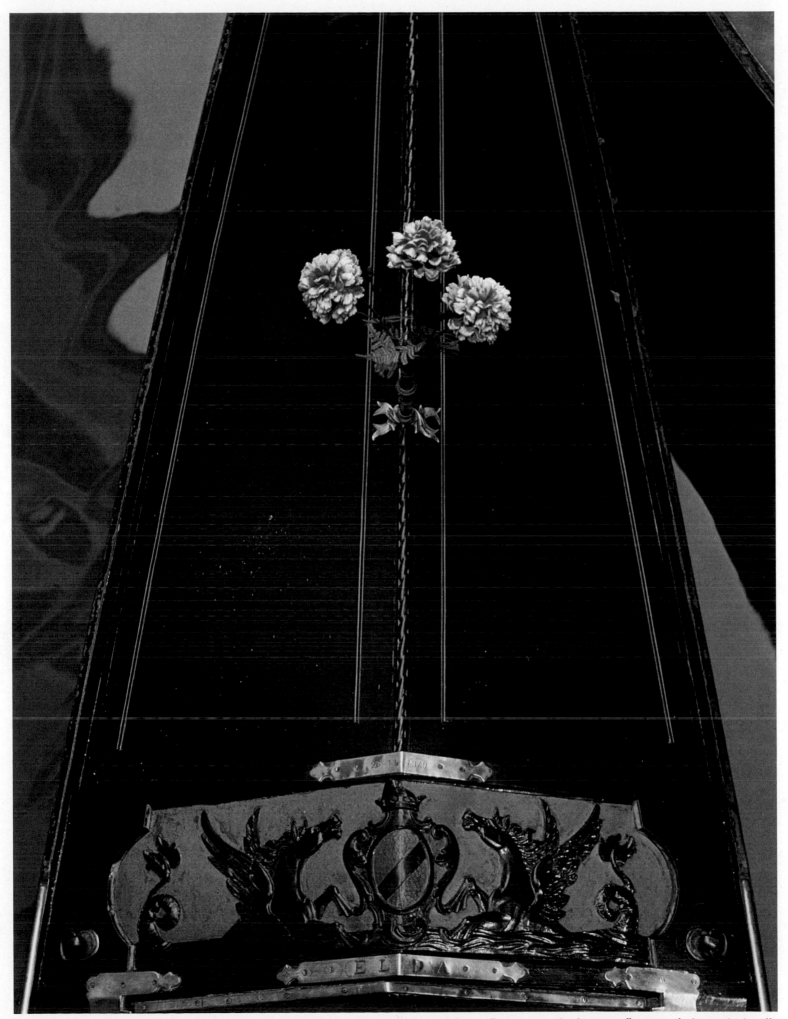

A heraldic crest and a polite-looking flower-vase decorate the narrow black hull of a gondola as it floats among the dancing reflections of adjacent high walls.

As black as their shadows, the people in St. Mark's Square look oddly two-dimensional against the sun-bleached pavement with its stippling of pigeons.

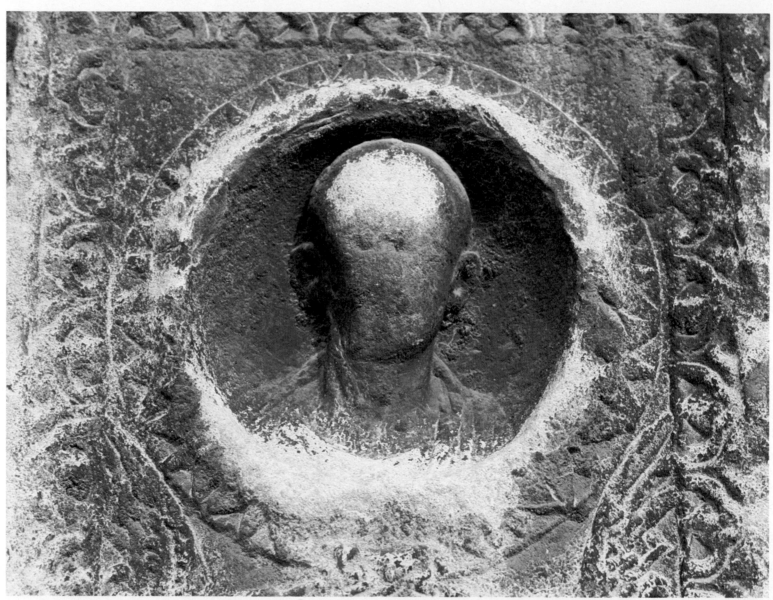

Set in a scratched and battered roundel and eroded beyond all recognition, a once-graceful sculptured head looks out with an indecipherable expression.

Fragments of three scenes on the island of Murano, reflected in mirrors hanging in a shop window, are outlined by the mirrors' scalloped and gilded frames.

A door curtain on Burano is draped to let the lagoon's sultry air circulate.

For a housewife who lives on the miniature waterfront of Burano, sitting on her own doorstep—feet extended—is equivalent to sitting at the water's edge.

Bibliography

Ackerman, James S., *Palladio.* Penguin Books, London, 1966.
Berengo, Marino, *La Società Veneta alla fine del Settecento.* Sansoni, Florence, 1956.
Berenson, Bernard, *Italian Pictures of the Renaissance: Venetian School.* Phaidon Press, London, 1957.
Bacchion, Eugenio, *The Basilica of St. Mark.* Ardo, Edizioni d'Arte, Venice, 1972.
Brion, Marcel, *Venice, the Masque of Italy.* Elek Books, London, 1962.
Burns, Howard, *Andrea Palladio 1508-1580.* The Arts Council of Great Britain, London, 1975.
Byron, Lord, *Letters of Lord Byron.* Everyman's Library. J. M. Dent & Sons, London, 1971.
Chambers, D. S., *The Imperial Age of Venice.* Thames and Hudson, London, 1970.
Davis, John H., *Venice.* Newsweek Book Division, New York, 1973.
Evelyn, John, *The Diary of John Evelyn.* Ed. William Bray, Everyman's Library, J. M. Dent & Sons, London, 1973.
Faure, Gabriel, *Venice.* Nicholas Kaye, London, 1957.
Goldoni, Carlo, *Four Comedies.* Penguin Books, London, 1968.
Goldoni, Carlo, *Memoirs of Carlo Goldoni.* Translated by John Black. A. A. Knopf, London, 1926.
Honour, Hugh, *The Companion Guide to Venice.* Collins, London, 1965.
Howells, W. D., *Venetian Life.* Houghton, Mifflin and Co., Boston, 1881.
International Fund for Monuments, *Venice in Peril.* Sansoni Editore, New York, 1970.

Istituto Veneto di Scienza, Lettere ed Arte, *Commissione di Studio per la Conservazione di Venezia.* 1968.
Kennard, J. S., *Goldoni and the Venice of his Time.* Macmillan Co., New York, 1920.
Links, J. G., *Venice.* Lutterworth, London, 1967.
Logan, Oliver, *Culture and Society in Venice 1470-1790.* B. T. Batsford, London, 1972.
Longworth, Philip, *The Rise and Fall of Venice.* Constable & Co., London, 1974.
Lorenzetti, Giulio, *Venice and its Lagoon.* Edizioni Lint, Trieste, 1975.
Lowe, Alfonso, *La Serenissima: the Last Flowering of the Venetian Republic.* Cassell & Co., London, 1974.
Luzzatto, Gino, *An Economic History of Italy.* Routledge & Kegan Paul, London, 1961.
McCarthy, Mary, *Venice Observed.* Penguin Books, London, 1972.
Maloney, F. J. Terence, *Glass in the Modern World.* Aldus Books, London, 1967.
Mannin, Ethel, *An Italian Journey.* Hutchinson and Co., London, 1974.
Mazzotti, Giuseppe, *Le Ville Venete.* Treviso, 1953.
Molmenti, P. G., *Venice: its individual growth from the earliest beginnings to the fall of the Republic* (6 vols.). Translated by Horatio F. Brown. John Murray, London, 1906-1908.
Morris, James, *Venice.* Faber & Faber Ltd., London, 1974.
Muraro, Michelangelo, *Invitation to Venice.* Paul Hamlyn, London, 1963.

Murray, Linda, *The High Renaissance.* Thames and Hudson, London, 1967.
Nicoll, Allardyce, *The World of Harlequin.* Cambridge University Press, 1963.
Pane, Roberto, *Palladio.* Einaudi, London, 1961.
Pignatti, Terisio, *Venice.* World Cultural Guide. Thames and Hudson, London, 1971.
Pirelli/Furlanis, *A System for Controlling the Water Level of the Venetian Lagoon.* Pirelli, Italy, 1975.
Pucci, Eugenio, *Venice—A Complete Guide for Visiting the City.* Bonechi, Florence, 1974.
Ruskin, John, *The Stones of Venice* (2 vols.). George Allen, 1886.
Shaw-Kennedy, Ronald, *Art and Architecture in Venice.* The Venice in Peril Guide. Sidgwick & Jackson, London, 1972.
Steer, John, *A Concise History of Venetian Painting.* Thames and Hudson, London, 1970.
Touring Club Italiano, *Venezia.* Milan, 1968.
UNESCO, *Rapporto su Venezia.* Paris-Milan, 1969.
Vasari, Giorgio, *The Lives of the Painters, Sculptors and Architects* (4 vols.). Translated by A. B. Hinds. Everyman's Library, J. M. Dent & Sons, London, 1970.
Wilde, Johannes, *Venetian Art from Bellini to Titian.* Clarendon Press, Oxford, 1974.
Williams, Jay, *The World of Titian.* Time-Life Books, Amsterdam, 1966.
Wittkower, Rudolf, *Art and Architecture in Italy 1600-1750.* Penguin Books, London, 1958.
Wittkower, Rudolf, *Studies in the Italian Baroque.* Thames and Hudson, London, 1975.

Acknowledgements and Picture Credits

The editors wish to thank the following: Giovanni Bresolin, Magistrato Alle Acque, Venice; Ente Provinciale del Turismo, Venice; Dr. Robin Cormack, Courtauld Institute of Art, London; Susie Dawson, London; Charles Dettmer, Thames Ditton, Surrey; Countess Teresa Foscari Foscolo, Italia Nostra, Venice; Ray Gardener, London; Baron Giambattista Rubin de Cervin, Director Museo Storico Navale, Venice; Jim Hicks, London; Lornie Leete-Hodge, Devizes, Wiltshire; J. G. Links, London; Russell Miller, London; Stuart Rossiter, London; Paolo Santillana, Venice; Deborah Sgardello, Rome; Paolo Selmi, State Archives, Venice; Professor Francesco Valconover, Superintendent, Soprintendenza alle Gallerie, Venice; Venice in Peril Fund, London; Mirko Vianello, City Council, Venice.

Sources for pictures in this book are shown below. Credits for the pictures from left to right are separated by commas; from top to bottom they are separated by dashes.

All photographs are by Ernst Haas except: Page 11—Giacomelli—Osvaldo Bohm. 34—Scala, Florence. 58—Ca'Rezzonico. 64—Bulloz, Paris courtesy of the Musée du Louvre, Paris. 87—Ernst Haas—Patrick Thurston, Ernst Haas. 103—Bonechi Editore, Florence. 106—courtesy of Museo Civico Correr, Venice, photo Scala, Florence. 122—Osvaldo Bohm, Scala, Florence. 123—Osvaldo Bohm. 124—Scala, Florence. 138—Patrick Thurston. 142—Roloff Beny. 146, 147—Roloff Beny. 151—Lou Klein—*I Quattro Libri del l'Architettura* by Andrea Palladio, 1642, Venice, by kind permission of the British Library Board. 156, 157—Erich Hartmann from Magnum. 162 to 165—Adam Woolfitt from Daily Telegraph Colour Library.

Index

Numerals in italics indicate a photograph or drawing of the subject mentioned.

A
Accademia, 121
Arsenale, 72
Art restoration, *99-101*
"Assumption" (Titian), *116-17*

B
Basilica: St. Mark's, 10, 12-13, 19, *30-1*, *32*, 39-43, *41*, *42*, *44-45*, 57, *80-1*, *96*, 102, *103*, 104, 107, *119*, *120*, 126, *130-2*, 171; bronze horses, 13, 16, 32, *44-5*, 88, *120*, 126; Pala d'Oro, *42*, 43, 126
Belisarius, 126
Bellini, Gentile, 107
Bellini, Giovanni, 95, 97, 98, 102, 104, 107, 118-19, 121, 122, *123*, 126, 127
Berenson, Bernard, 170
Bienniale, 81, 95-7, 127, 129
Bissone, *70-6*
Brenta Canal, 145, 148-153
Bridges: of Sighs, 36, 38, 118; Rialto, 10
Burano, island of, *158-9*, *176-7*, 178-9, *196-7*
Buoninsegna, Gian Paolo, 43
Byron, Lord, 7, 89-90, 92-3, 117, 118
Byzantine art and architecture, 12, 33, 39-43, *41*, *42*, 47, *52-3*, 102-3, *120*, 171, 178

C
Cafés, *see* Florian's, Quadri's
Calle della Malvasia, *60-1*
Cambrai, League of, 127
Campanile, *4*, *10-11*, 19, *34*, *132-3*, *136-7*, 170
Campo San Giovanni and San Paolo,

Canals, 6, 7, *8-9*, 10, 14, 16, 18, *60-1*, *108-111*, *141-2*, *see also* Grand Canal
Canaletto, 127
Caorline, *68-9*, 77
Carpaccio, Vittore, 34
Cavallini, Pietro, 42, 103
Chagall, Marc, 97
Chioggia, *162-3*; War of, 126
Churches: Church of the Jesuits, 126; Il Redentore, 127, 170-1, *182-3*; San Pantalon, 100; San Zaccaria, 118; Santa Fosca, 178; Santa Maria dei Frari, *116-17*; Santa Maria della Salute, *6-7*, *8-9*, 10, 127
Cicisbei, 65-6
Cimabue, Giovanni, 42-3, 103
Colleoni, Bartolomeo, statue of, 18, 128, 143-4, *145*
Commedia dell'Arte, *58-9*, 63, 97
Condottieri, 143-4
Contarini, Marino, 127
Correr Civic Museum, *94-5*
Croce, Benedetto, 170
Crusade, Fourth, 13, 16, 41, 126

D
Dali, Salvador, 119

da Gama, Vasco, 38-9, 127
d'Amadio, Marco, 127
da Messina, Antonello, 98, *106*, 106-7
da Vinci, Leonardo, 98, 104, 106, 121
del Verrocchio, Andrea, 144, *145*
de Mille, Cecil B., 126
Doges, 32-4, 36, 43, *85*, 126, 128, 143, 163, 170, 184
Doges' Palace, 6, 10, 32-3, *34-5*, 36, *36-7*, *38-9*, 39, 40, 57, *124*, 127, *135*
Duccio di Buoninsegna, 42-3, 103

E
Emperors: Diocletian, *96*; Justinian, 126

F
"Feast at the House of Levi" (Veronese), 129
Fellini, Federico, 85
Festivals: Bienniale, 81, 95-7, 127, 129; Film, 82, 84-5, 88; Il Redentore, 170-1; Regatta, *68-79*
Florian's Café, 12, 88
Fondaco dei Tedeschi, 125
Foscari family, *85*, *104-5*, *150-1*
Fresco, *see* painting techniques

G
Gauguin, Paul, 98
Giorgione da Castelfranco, 95, 97, 98, 103, 119, 121, *122*, 125, 126
Giotto, 42-3, 103
Glassmaking, 145, *180-1*, 180-4
"Golden Book", 32-3, 36, 126
Goldoni, Carlo, 57-67, *59*, 81, 127, 148, 184
Gondolas, 6-7, 10, 62, 71, *78-9*, *86-7*, *108-9*, *111*, *190-1*
Gondoliers, 7, 10, *16-17*, *60-1*, 62, 67, *68-79*
Gothic architecture, 32, 39, *50*, *104-5*, *116-17*, 127
Grado, island of, 126
Grand Canal, 7, *8-9*, 10, 16, 18-19, 31, 58, 62-3, 69, 70, *71*, 85-6, *87*, *104-5*, 118, 125, 143, 153, 155, 175, 187
Gritti Palace, 19
Guardi, Francesco, 127
Giudecca Canal, 170-1
Giudecca, island of, 170-1, *182-3*
Great Council, 33, 36, *38*, 126

H
Halls, in Doges' Palace: of the Great Council, 36, *38-9*; of the Senate, 36; of the Strong Box, 36; of the Ten, 36
Horses, statues of, *see* Basilica St. Mark's

I
Islands, *see* Burano, Giudecca, Grado, Lido, Murano, Poveglia, Rialto, San Lazzaro, San Michele, Torcello
Italians, character of, 171, 174

L
Lacemaking, *158-9*, *176-7*, 179
Lagoon, *14-15*, 118, *155-6*, *164-5*, *166-7*,

168-9
La Fenice, 57-8, *62*, 62-3, 65-7, 81
"La Malcontenta", 149, *150-1*
La Serenissima, 70
Lepanto, Battle of, 127
Lido, The, 82-5, 117, 145, *157*
Loren, Sophia, 5-7
Lysippus, 16

M
"Madonna in Glory" (Duccio), 42
"Madonna and Child with Four Saints" (Bellini), 118, 121, *123*
Malipiero family, *175*
Mann, Thomas, 83-4
Map of Venice, *14-15*
Marghera, *112-13*, *166-7*, *172-3*, 174-5, 179, 187
"Martyrdom of St. Lawrence" (Titian), 126
Mestre, 175
Michelangelo Buonarroti, 98, 125, 170, 175
Mocenigo, Doge, 170
Modigliani, 102
Molo San Marco, 16
Mosaics, in St. Mark's, 41-3, *44-55*, 102-4, *103*
Motoscafi, *8-9*, 86
Murano, island of, 145, *180-1*, 182, 184, *195*
Mussolini, Benito, 81, 171, 174

N
Napoleon Bonaparte, 16, 32, 127, 161

O
Oil-painting, *see* painting techniques

P
Painting techniques: fresco, 104, 106; oils, 98, 106-7; tempera, 104, 106
Pala d'Oro, *42*, 43, 126, 182
Palazzi: Ca d'Oro, 127; Cent'Anni, 59; Dandolo, 118; Zoscari, *85*, *104-5*; Gritti, 19; **Palladio, Andrea,** 127, *146-7*, 148-153, 170-1, 182
Pantalone, *58*, 58, 59, 60, 67
Picasso, Pablo, 59, 95, 97
"Pietà" (Antonello da Messina), *106*
Pisani family, 152
Polo, Marco, 88, 126, 175
Pope Julius II, 98
Portuguese, 38-9
Poveglia, island of, *168-9*
Procuratie Nuove, *5*

Q
Quadri's Café, *119*

R
Regatta, *68-79*
Renaissance architecture, 12, 184, 127
Retro-Venice, 16, 18, 175
Rialto, 6, *14-15*, 126, 148

S
St. Mark, 7, 10, 16, *34-5*, *103*, 103

St. Mark's, *see* Basilica
St. Mark's Square, *4*, 10, *12-13*, 12-13, *20-9*, *83*, 88, 117, *119*, *131-9*, 144, 184, *192-3*
San Lazzaro, island of, *155-6*
San Michele, island of, *161-2*
Sansovino Library, 127
Scuola di San Rocco, 129, 170
Scuole, 102
Shelley, Percy Bysshe, 89
Statues: Colleoni, 18, 128, 143-4, *145*; Tetrarchs, *96*
Stucco, 152

T
Tempera, *see* painting techniques
"Tempest, The" (Giorgione), 121, *122-3*
Tiepolo, Gian Domenico, *64-5*
Tiepolo, Giovanni Battista, 127
Tintoretto, 36, *38*, 95, 97, 98, 126, 127, 129
Titian, 36, 95, 96-7, 98, *117*, 121, *122*, 125, 127, 174
Togliatti, 174

Torcello, island of, 126, *175*, 178
Tourists, *see* Venice
Tree of Liberty, 184
"Triumph of Venice" (Tintoretto), 36
"Triumph of Venice" (Veronese), *124*, 127

U
UNESCO, 127

V
Van Gogh, Vincent, 98
Vaporetti, 86
Vasari, Giorgio, 125
Veneziano, Paolo, 7
Venice: architecture of, 6, 7, 10, 12, 21, 32, 145, 148-153; art, 41-3, 95-8, 102-7, 118-19, 121-9; chronology of, 126-7; climate of, 82; commerce, 38, *86-7*, 184; early invaders, 31; families of, *see* Foscari, Malipiero, Pisani; first cathedral of, 178; floods, *21-8*, 99, 127, *184-5*; food, 117; founding of, 31, 126; foundations of, 31, 169; future of, 99, 171, 174, 186; government of, 31-3, 36; history of, 31-3, 38-9, 126-7, 178, 184; inhabitants of, 18, *56-7*, 57-8, 88-92, 170; La Serenissima, 70; map of, *14-15*; present dangers, 153, 169; theatre, *see* Commedia dell'Arte, La Fenice, Goldoni; tourists, 12, 81, 83, 86, 89, 117, *130-141*, 148-9, 152-3, 175, 178; visitors to, 89, 118
Venturi, Adolfo, 170
Veronese, Paolo, *38*, 95, 97, 122, *124*, 126-9, 142-3, 174, 184
Victor Emmanuel, King, 127
Villas, 145-153; Caldogno, *146-7*; La Malcontenta, 149, *150-1*; Barbaro, *142-3*
Visconti, Luchino, 84

W
Worthy Ones, The, 32-3, 36, 38, 66, 97, 126, 128, 143-5, 148, 150-2, 187

Z
"Zanipolo", *see* Campo San Giovanni and San Paolo

Colour reproduction by Irwin Photography Ltd., at their Leeds PDI Scanner Studio.
Filmsetting by C. E. Dawkins (Typesetters) Ltd., London, SE1 1UN.
Printed and bound in Italy by Arnoldo Mondadori, Verona.